RESCUE *Smiles*

FAVORITE ANIMAL STORIES OF LOVE AND LIBERATION

EDITED BY HEATHER LEUGHMYER AND TAMIRA THAYNE

Published by Who Chains You Publishing
P.O. Box 581
Amissville, VA 20106
www.WhoChainsYou.com

ISBN-10: 1-946044-10-5
ISBN-13: 978-1-946044-10-5

Printed in the United States of America

First Edition

*To all the fur critters
we've known and loved.
Thank you for showing us
the meaning of unconditional love.*

Also from Who Chains You Books

✦

Foster Doggie Insanity: Tips and Tales to Keep your Kool
as a Doggie Foster Parent

A Doggie Hero is Born

The Wrath of Dog

Rescue Smiles: Favorite Animal
Stories of Love and Liberation

The Puppy Who Left Puddles on the Floor

It's About A Dog

Honey's Second Chance

Emma's Second Chance

Richard "Bugman" Fagerlund: My Path to the Bugman

If Your Tears Were Human

Adopting Adele

The Dog Thief and Other Stories

The Listener's Tale

And More! Visit us at WhoChainsYou.Com

Contents

THE BANDIT AND THE ENGINEER: ALICE 1

THE BEAUTY OF RESCUE: UNA, THE BIGGEST ISH 13

HOME AT LAST: SARGE 25

HEART OF A RAT: SABRE 37

IN THE BEGINNING: BLUE AND RANGER 43

COMING IN FROM THE COLD: MISTY 52

FOR THE LOVE OF BLIND DOGS: DIMITRI 58

MIND OF A MOUSE: PEZ 63

EVERLASTING LOVE: HOPE 67

INSEPARABLE SURPRISES: CISSY AND MISSY 77

CATALYSTS FOR CHANGE: CINNAMON AND SPICE 81

HER GIFT TO ME: MISS RAT 88

Dying to Live: Gene-O 94

Uncompromised Compassion: Layla, Ricky,

and Lucy 97

A Feral Princess: Bootsie, aka Tootance 101

And All Things Nice: Cinnamon and Sugar 105

Finding Sanctuary: Von Truman 122

No More Chains: Gator 129

The Church Ladies: Lonestar and Tejas 138

Sparrow in the House: Birdie................................. 150

THE BANDIT AND THE ENGINEER:
Alice

BY LAURA KOERBER

Stray

THE LITTLE DOG CROUCHED beneath the tangle of blackberries and salal and waited. The man banged the front door open, strode across the lawn, and flung himself into his SUV. The brake lights flashed, the engine hummed, and the car rolled backward into the street where it reoriented itself and vanished in a puff of exhaust.

She wrinkled her nose: bad smell. Then she waited. The door opened and a woman hurtled out. She had her arms full of stuff, which she dumped on the hood of her car while she fished for her keys. Then she looked over toward the little dog under the rhody. They made eye contact. The little dog tensed, but this eye contact was part of the morning routine. Then the woman flung her stuff into the car, slid in, and blasted off in a swirl of noise and exhaust fumes.

The two people left at the same time every weekday morning. The little dog knew their routine because she had been watching them for months. She didn't know the names of the days of the week, but she knew the pattern of days when they departed early in the morning and days when they didn't.

As soon as the woman's car was out of sight, the little dog emerged from the brush, scurried across the street, and dived into the safety of the forsythia hedge. She burrowed through the side yard shrubbery and popped out into the backyard where she was greeted by the moist smell of food. In one bound she was up on the deck and had her nose in the bowl.

The food was there every morning, and if she was quick, she got to eat it all. If she wasn't quick, the cat got it first. Sometimes the crows got it. The crows she could chase off, but the cat was downright mean. She gobbled and snuffled with one eye out for the ferocious beast; but luckily, there was no cat today.

She stepped back from the bowl, licking her lips. What else could she find on the deck?

Water—there was always water in the bowl. The cat didn't drink much, and didn't mind sharing. The little dog was thirsty so she drank deeply. Then she had a quick look around.

Some bags of something that smelled nasty (fertilizer),

a large potted plant that the cat had peed on, the smell of the human and cat on the doormat, and the scent of human on a pair of shoes. She sniffed carefully. She liked the warm human smell. She picked one shoe up. The fabric was soft in her mouth (canvas deck shoe). It had a sharp taste, very human (sweat).

She ran with the shoe in her mouth around the house, across the street, and into her private passageway through the berry canes and salal of the undeveloped lots. She felt safe in the comforting embrace of the forest. Her pace slowed. She had to hold her head up high to keep the shoe from snagging on the ferns and forest litter. She stopped by a fallen tree. The roots, ripped out of the ground, formed an immense fan shape, and were overgrown with moss and ferns. At the bottom of the fan in the dirt was a hollow which she had enlarged and deepened. She dropped the shoe into the hollow.

A fat drop of rain struck her one upraised ear. She heard the singing of the rain in the treetops; then she felt a wet sting on her nose. She wriggled down into her burrow.

It took awhile for her to rearrange the shoes to her satisfaction. She did this every time she returned to her borrow; pawed and stirred the shoes around, pushing them this way and that. It stirred up the human smell, which she loved. The shoes reminded her of her childhood. Once she had lived in a house, and had been warm and dry with food and water available whenever she was hungry or thirsty. Once, people had provided that warmth and the food and water for her. Then the people went away and she learned to live outside and to find food, water and warmth for herself.

She didn't remember the people at all, though she

remembered the home and the smell of people, the smell that went with food and water and warmth and safety. She snuggled down into the shoes to wait out the rain. Later she would venture out again. There were other decks and porches with bowls of food. She was lonely, but she always got enough to eat.

Dinnertime

Thomas unlocked his front door, hung his coat in the closet, slipped his loafers off his feet, and dropped his briefcase onto the floor by the hat tree. Balancing precariously on first on foot and then the other, he put on his slippers. They were a gift from his sister, and he felt an obligation to wear them everyday.

He checked the clock; it was six forty-one. He usually got home by six-thirty, but this day he had needed to stop for gas. He usually bought gas on the way to work, but for some reason, the dial had dropped to a quarter tank on the way home. He never let the car get below one-quarter tank; but he liked to buy gas on the way to work, not on the way home. The dilemma had made a misery of his drive: stop for gas or not? Stopping for gas had won out, but now he was afraid that his whole routine had changed and from now on he would be buying gas on the way home and not in the morning. He didn't mind change so much; he just didn't like it when change happened unexpectedly, in an unplanned way.

But now it was dinnertime. Thomas had a big bowl of salad already made up, and he had frozen lasagna waiting for him in the freezer, which would meet his need for nutrition.

He placed some grapes in a bowl, nuked the lasagna, added the salad to the edge of the plate, and sat down in front of the TV to eat.

But he didn't watch the TV. He had a planned change of routine. He was reading books about dog care: *The Complete Owner's Guide for Dog Lovers, The Encyclopedia of Major Dog Breeds,* and *Dog Behavior Training for Idiots.* (His sister had given him that as one of her jokes because she knew he was really, really smart, but not at things like dog care).

He opened the *Complete Owner's Guide* and began to read.

Trapped

The bowl was inside a wire box covered with a towel. She had never seen such a thing. Why was the food in a den? She liked the den, at least she liked the idea of dens, but she wasn't sure why the food was in this den when it had never been in a den before.

The humans had left for the morning as usual. She was there, right on time, beating the cat to the food once again. It was the same food as usual (she could tell by the smell). But for some reason the humans had put the food in a den. (She knew the humans put the food out. She thought they put it out for the cat. It never occurred to her that they might be putting the food out for her).

She was awfully hungry. Maybe it didn't matter if the food was in a den. It was raining again and she was wet. The inside of the den was dry.

She poked her head into the den. Nothing bad happened. She stepped in. Nothing bad happened.

She jumped in the rest of the way in and sank her face into the food bowl, gobbling greedily. Then something bad happened; a clang of metal on metal.

She whirled around in a panic. The den had closed up. She flung herself against the wire. That hurt. But what else could she do? She tried again, slamming her side against the hard metal wires, but the wires didn't give. She tried biting and scratching. She tried body slamming again.

It was useless. She was stuck.

Kennel

The little dog cowered at the back of the kennel. It was like the den on the deck, only bigger—a lot bigger, actually. There was a warm dry inside part with a soft place for sleeping, and a dry but not warm part outside that had wire sides and front and a roof. There was a bucket of water and a bucket of food, more food than she could eat.

She liked the inside part of the kennel. She had some of her shoe collection with her.

She kept her shoes piled up on her bed.

She didn't like the outside part of the kennel because unfamiliar people were always walking by. Sometimes they tried to talk to her through the wires. Sometimes they came right into the kennel. When they invaded her territory, she barked at them, which usually made them go away.

She recognized certain people now. Certain people came into the kennel and left food and water, changed the blankets on the bed, and picked up her poop. She was getting used to those familiar people. She knew they weren't going to hurt her. She didn't like them, though; she didn't really trust them.

One a day a person came in and put a leash on her and made her go outside to a big grassy field with other dogs. She ran around the edges of the field and checked out every inch of the fence. The big grassy field was boring. With no way to escape, she had no interest in being out in the rain. She didn't mind the other dogs, but didn't play with them. They approached her, sniffed, and then left her alone.

Being dragged out to the field became a daily routine. The only thing she liked about the big grassy area was when one of the people would throw a ball. She liked to chase the ball. It wasn't really like the small animals she sometimes hunted and ate, but the ball did run away, and it was fun to chase. And if she brought it back, the human would give her a treat and throw the ball again, so she could chase it again.

It felt good to run. She was never hungry any more because there was always food. And she slept really well, even though she didn't have all of her shoes. The kennel smelled like humans. It was like being a puppy again, but it was kind of boring.

Sometimes she wondered if she would ever be able to go back to her hollow in the forest with the rest of her shoe collection. She liked having food and water and being warm and she liked chasing the ball, but she didn't like being bored and being stared at.

Preparation

To the staff at Save-a-Pet,

I am writing this on behalf of my brother, who would

like to meet the dog you call "Alice", the Jack Russell terrier mix. You describe her as odd, quirky, and unsocialized to people or dogs. That's not a bad description of my brother. He, too, is odd, quirky and unsocialized to others, but he is a kind person and has a warm heart. My brother has Asperger's Syndrome. He knows that he has difficulty socializing with people. That's part of why he would like to adopt a dog, and it's why he would like to meet Alice. Please let me know when we can make an appointment with your adoption counselor.

Thank you, Elizabeth

"There's someone coming to meet you, Alice." They had dumped her in a bathtub, sprayed her with hot water, scrubbed her with soap until her smell was gone, and pummeled her with towels. Alice was not in a good mood. She let her feelings be known by hunching her back, tucking her tail and glowering.

"Oh you are so pretty; even if you only have one ear." One of the humans slid her hand over Alice's head and down her back. Alice did not acknowledge the pat. It felt good to be touched, but she had not yet forgiven the humans for the bath.

"I hope you can like him," said the human. "He's an engineer; a very smart man with plenty of money to take care of you, and who lives in his own house in the Heights neighborhood. You will be able to see all over the city from his windows."

The human sounded a bit wistful, as if she would like to live in a house on the Heights. She stroked Alice's one big ear. "I wonder what happened to your other ear? Well, it doesn't matter." The human stood up briskly. "Here's a treat, my dear, and try not to be grumpy, OK?"

Alice snapped the tossed treat out of the air.

The humans wandered off to the office and left Alice to roam the lobby area on her own. She sniffed the corners; other dogs had peed there, but Alice didn't like to pee on hard surfaces that splashed back. There was a bag of treats on the counter, but she wasn't tall enough to reach them, even if she stood on her tiptoes. She tried anyway, but she couldn't even get halfway up the counter. She could get on a chair, though, and she knew from previous visits to the lobby that some of the chairs were very soft.

Alice jumped up into an overstuffed chair and curled up. She watched the door. Something was going on, she could tell. Something was about to happen to her.

Meeting

Thomas stared across the room at the dog, and the dog stared back.

He said, "She's kind of funny looking with just one ear." The photo on the website had been a profile of the side with an ear. It was false advertising to mislead people into thinking a dog had two ears when she only had one.

The adoption counselor said, "It looks like her ear got bitten or cut off. We don't know what experiences she had while she was living on her own, but obviously some of the experiences were bad. She's not very trusting of people. In fact, we had to trap her to catch her."

"She was a stray?" Elizabeth asked.

"She lived in the woods next to the Firwood Hills development. Do you know where I mean, out in Richmond?"

"Way out there?"

"Yes, we were contacted by some people who had been trying to make friends with her for a long time. They were feeding her on their deck. They told us that she was sort of a neighborhood dog and everyone knew about her, but she wouldn't let anyone get close to her. They called her the Shoe Bandit because she was always stealing shoes and things like that off peoples' decks."

Elizabeth laughed. Thomas didn't. He asked why she wanted peoples' shoes.

The counselor shrugged. "I don't know, but they told us that she lived in a cave she dug under a log and her den was full of peoples' shoes. In fact, she has some of these shoes here with her. The people who helped us trap her showed us her den, so we brought some of her shoes along with her. She sleeps with them like they're stuffed toys or something."

"Can we take some with her if Thomas adopts her?" Elizabeth asked.

"Sure. I think you should. She will need something familiar."

A silence fell. The humans were standing at one end of the lobby and Alice was standing at the other. The counselor said, "Let's see if you can make friends with her."

Thomas and Alice stared at each other. Neither one knew what to do.

"I'll take you out to the playfield and show you how to play ball with her," said the counselor.

Ball

Thomas played ball with Alice every day at six forty-five. He walked her in the morning at seven o'clock, and dropped her off at doggie day care at ten minutes past eight. He picked her up again at six fifteen and got home by six forty-five. They always played catch with a pink foam football immediately after getting out of the car. The ball rested on the front porch. Alice always ran to get the ball and brought it to Thomas. He loved the fierce enthusiasm in her face when she brought her ball, her one ear erect and vibrating like an antenna, her eyes alight, her tail a blur of wags. It made his heart lift.

He threw the ball with big wind-milling movements of his arms. It felt good to him to make large muscle group movements, but the ball often did not go where he intended. She always started running as soon as the ball was in his hand. She was a great wide receiver, checking over her shoulder to gauge the arc of the ball in flight, and leaping up to snatch it out of the air, landing on her feet at a dead run.

They were the sight of the neighborhood. No one minded her running across their grass or out into the street. People waved and yelled, "That's a good one! Great catch, Alice!"

They entered their house together, united in pride.

Update

Thomas sent an email update to the dog rescue. He wrote:

As far as I can tell, Alice is adapting well to life as

prescribed by the dog care manual I have been studying. She eats a cup and a half of sweet potato and fish dog food each day. She defecates during our morning walk and never has accidents in the house. She likes to sit next to me on the couch. We are watching football together. Attached are some photographs which I hope you will display on the bulletin board at your facility."

Photos

A series of photos are pinned to the bulletin board now. One shows Alice eating from a white ceramic bowl with her name on it in red. Another shows a dog bed on the floor next to the human's bed. The dog bed is full of shoes. The last photo shows Thomas and Alice, both wearing 49ers jerseys, sitting next to each other on a couch. There's a bag of popcorn next to Thomas and a bag of dog treats next to Alice.

Alice looks bemused, as if she isn't quite sure what happened to her life. Thomas looks like he is trying to be a sports fan. They both look happy, sort of.

This is a true story.

⊙⊙

Laura Koerber is an artist and writer who lives on an island with her husband and her two dogs. Her first book, *The Dog Thief and Other Stories* (written as Jill Kearney), was listed by Kirkus Review as one of the One Hundred Best Books of 2015. She's also the author of *The Listener's Tale, The Shapeshifter's Tale, Limbo,* and *I Once Was Lost, But Now I'm Found.*

THE BEAUTY OF RESCUE:
Una, the Biggest Ish

by TAMIRA THAYNE

The Ditch Kitty

I GAZED RELUCTANTLY at the cat as he looked out at me from the confines of his carrier. He was still young, and gray with an apple face, big green eyes, and snot bubbles oozing and then abating with each rattling breath.

Somehow it was that last part that captured all of my attention.

It was the left nostril, to be exact; the one that oozed.

His left eye leaked, too, but at least that fluid was clear, and not of immediate concern.

I sighed. "I'll take him, Mary."

Mary's shoulders sagged in relief. "Thank you. I just can't afford one more sick animal to care for. The last two have wiped me out financially."

Mary lived in a rundown house in a small, equally decrepit central Pennsylvania town. The drywall was ripped completely off the studs in the entry room, either from her rescue dogs working "construction" (or, more accurately, "destruction"), or her on-again-off-again husband's attempts to renovate. I was afraid to ask, so I just acted like nothing was awry when I stepped in out of the cold.

Mary had a caring heart, though, and she really did try to help the pitiful animals who came her way—unlike a lot of other folk I dealt with in the area. Her house was clean, and she worked a full-time job at the grocery store in town, trying to make ends meet while her husband spent most of his paltry wages propped up at the bar in the Elks Club a few blocks over.

She was not a complainer, but her face told me more than she let on. She was overwhelmed, and probably wondered daily if this was all there would ever be to her life. I hoped not.

She had come across the cat sitting in a ditch near her home—most-likely abandoned by a local ne'er-do-well when he came down with the sickness—and due to the presence of the aforementioned heart of gold, she couldn't leave him there.

I wouldn't have been able to either, truth be told.

She called and asked if I'd take the cat because I ran an animal non-profit, and she hoped the organization could pay to fix him up and find him a new home. Trouble was, my non-profit was geared toward chained dogs, and our policy on taking in and vetting cats—after being inundated with both cats and requests to take more cats—had evolved into "worst-case scenario" ONLY.

There were no exceptions.

Except today.

I sighed again. I guess this guy qualified under worst-case scenario, anyway. He *was* pretty sickly, and I just couldn't say "No" to either him or Mary. I didn't have it in me.

I gathered him up, cat carrier and all, and we made our way back down the 30-mile stretch of highway toward my home and the base of my rescue operation.

He was too ill to protest the drive, and I was left alone with dreams of a day when the need wasn't so crushing. That day would not be today.

The Cat Gets a Name

The kids and I decided to name him Charlie, a named picked by my daughter because she'd loved and lost a gray female cat named Charlotte.

I tend to be a nickname evolver, starting at one name and adding onto it or changing it as I go (the sillier the better so as to get a giggle out of the kids). It wasn't long before I had elaborated on his given name, calling him Charlie Tuna after the Star-Kist commercials of my youth.

My son was nine when Charlie came to live with us, and my daughter only three, so they hadn't seen the same commercials I had. But they were all too willing to play along with a name that sounded wackadoodle to them. They'd chortle just thinking of a cat that was named after a fish.

My youngest couldn't wrap her tongue around the name Charlie Tuna, though, or really most complicated words yet at that point in her speech development.

Charlie Tuna's name soon evolved to Tuna, the Biggish Fish—which Brynnan simply couldn't pronounce—so she instead called him Una, the Biggest Ish.

That name stuck.

Bad News

Una, the Biggest Ish (see, it does have a certain ring to it) and I spent a lot of time at the vet's office in those early months. The first antibiotic seemed to take effect—he showed a lessening in levels of snot production and eye waterworks at least—so we gave him his required shots and soon had his dangly bits removed.

But our progress was short-lived, and soon Tuna was sicker than ever. Even worse, two more of the immune-compromised cats who lived with us came down with the sickness too. We tried every antibiotic on the market, and not a one of them worked long-term. We'd have some initial success with a few of them, but soon we were back to the drawing board.

I didn't know what to do, and I felt frustrated and helpless on where to go from here.

I put the word out to my fellow rescuers asking for advice on our discussion boards (this was before social media) and many recommended a raw food diet to build his immune system and allow him to fight off the illness himself.

To say this solution was distasteful to me would have been putting it mildly. I was a few years into vegetarianism by then, so the mere thought of cutting up and grinding raw chicken for my cats disgusted me. I didn't even cook meat for my kids! And now I'd have to shop for it, buy it, and cut it up raw every week for my cats?

Ugh.

I thought about it long and hard before committing to taking that step, but in the end I believed I had to try it to save the kitties' lives. If there was a chance it would work, I had to take it.

I bought a meat grinder (don't get me started!), and for the next year I chopped organic chicken, ground up bones, and added eggs and all manner of necessary cat vitamins and nutrients to make the raw food diet nutritionally complete for the cats who were sick.

In order to make sure Tuna didn't get into any dry cat food, I was forced to move ALL the cats to a raw food diet. Rest assured, not a one of them complained about the raw gunk they noshed and gnawed on, but I sure did!

A survey of all cats in the household confirmed that they preferred the raw food diet by a margin of 5-0. At least someone was happy.

I lasted a year with it.

To my surprise and delight, by the end of a year, Una, the Biggest Ish (and the others, too) were well enough to go off the diet! I had a long talk with the members of my cat household about the end of their raw food extravaganza, and although they were not in favor, the dictator who paid for their food won in the end.

I broke up with the raw food diet. It was a glorious day—at least for me.

I was sorry they were going to be stuck with nasty dry food again—for which I apologized in advance—but I'd taken all I could take. The rest was on them.

A Most Unusual Kitty

I was always a cat lover (although I oddly ended up in dog rescue), and I have met and cohabitated with many felines since my youth. Shortly after bringing the snot-nosed kitty into my life, I would realize something that I still know to be true today: he was and is the most unique cat I'd ever have the pleasure of sharing my home with.

Although I enjoy the signature qualities that make cats cats—the mystery, standoffishness, and self-sufficiency they all carry to a certain degree—Una, by contrast, is much more like a dog than a cat in temperament.

He looks me in the eye when he "talks" to me, sleeps directly on my head with his face on my cheek, and he often and to this day eats his food by picking it up with his paws and bringing it to his mouth instead of just biting it.

He insists on drinking water from the sink, and loudly protests if you don't turn it on for him upon demand. He also sleeps in the sink—but only if it's dry—which means after he drinks he has to move to another sink to lie in.

I've trained him to go sit where I point, so if he's sitting on the counter, I can point to the toilet seat and he'll jump onto it and look at me expectantly.

Because then he's waiting for his kitty brushing….which means I pick up my brush (don't tell my husband) and brush the fur on his face, back, and sides with it. He is, in fact, so impatient for his grooming that he jumps up and grabs the brush with both paws and pushes it onto his face himself. I giggle and tell him to be patient, I'm getting to it. Patience is not one of his virtues.

He lets himself out the doggie door downstairs, and knocks at the front door upstairs when he wants back in.

I believe he could have been trained for and done well in an animal act—he's that smart and responsive to humans—but alas, I wouldn't subject him to anything that might go against his best interests, and he just couldn't join the traveling circus without me anyway. He's my baby.

Too bad I never trained him to do really cool things myself. I always meant to…

He Wouldn't Open His Mouth

One of my favorite Una anecdotes is recent, and reflects more on my husband's lack of feline understanding that the perfection of all that is Una.

When my shepherd, Sloan, was still alive, I gave him a liquid supplement every day that was supposed to help his joints, eyes, and fur. Although it provided him with a higher quality of life up until the end, the day still came that we had to say goodbye; I hate that part.

After Sloan passed away, I still had bottles of the rather-expensive supplement left in my cupboard, and I remembered it was supposed to be good for cats too. With Una aging, I decided to give him a dose of it each morning to help stave off the inevitable decline and parting that I know will come sooner rather than later.

He quickly, and in his usual smart-kitty fashion, decided he quite liked the taste of BioCell, and started "requesting" it loudly each morning.

I called it his Num Num Dumb Dumbs, just so I could say "Una, you want your Num Num Dumb Dumbs?" And, because I knew if I asked him if he wanted his Num Num Dumb Dumbs he'd soon associate it with the medicine and come running for it.

I was right. Now as soon as I get out of bed and go out to the kitchen, he meanders in and jumps onto the end barstool closest to the refrigerator, yapping until the Num Nums are produced. He's not really picky about which human slave is doling out the Num Nums, by the way, but he insists that someone better be anteing up and pronto!

He gets about ¼ teaspoon of the solution daily by dropper, which I use to push open the side of his mouth and squeeze the supplement in.

Since he actually enjoys the flavor of the Num Nums, he's not resistant to it (extremely rare for a cat), and passively allows me to prop open his mouth with the dropper, swallowing as I squeeze it onto the back of his tongue.

Then I drop a little onto the counter for him to lick afterward, which helps him remember that he willingly takes the vitamin mix because it's apparently tasty enough to entice even a cat. Who knew that was possible?

One day I wasn't home for the morning ritual, and when

I came home later I asked my hubby if he had given Una his Num Nums. His response?

"I tried, but he wouldn't open his mouth."

Whaaa-at?! My jaw fell slack. I could picture how it went down in my head—Joe standing there with the dropper in his hand and pleading with Tuna to open up, baffled and confused when the cat just stared back at him.

Una, on the other hand, was probably thinking to himself, "Why did Mom let this oaf in charge of Num Nums? Obviously, we're gonna need to have a talk about replacing him."

I tried not to laugh...too hard. "Honey, Una's smart and all, and he's unusual, but he's not COMPLETELY human! He doesn't just open his mouth on command for you to dish out the supplement like you're feeding pureed pears to a baby."

Needless to say, Joe has been in remedial cat training for husbands ever since "the episode".

He did proudly announce recently that he'd successfully given Una his Num Nums while I was away.

Una is Gone, Take One

Una used to love to go on walks up the driveway with Sloan and me. We are blessed to live on 35 wooded acres out in the countryside of Virginia, and our driveway winds down a half mile of gravel road, lined on both sides by forest and fields.

Sloan had slowed down quite a bit by that last year, so Una could generally keep up with us as we crawled up the hill, and then slowly made our way back down again to the house.

I had seen a coyote on my wildlife camera, and regularly

had foxes, raccoons, and even bears make cameos on film as well. On this particular day, I felt sure that Una was lumbering about 100 yards behind Sloan and I as we crested the rise and walked to our usual turnaround point.

But when I turned around to go down the hill, I couldn't see Una anywhere; he'd just disappeared! I berated myself for not watching him better, and called for him as I tried not to devolve into a state of panic on my way back to the house. Nonetheless, I was in a bit of a frenzy by the time I reached my front door, and burst into the living room, asking Joe if he'd seen my kitty.

Joe isn't quite the animal lover that I am, but he's pretty supportive in an emergency situation, and he knows how much I love that cat; so he hopped up, threw on his shoes, and off we went back up the hill to look for Una.

As soon as we got to where I'd lost him, I heard an animal screaming off in the woods to our left. Oh God! Had the coyote grabbed Tuna? There's no way my cat could survive that! He's a big boy, but he's really just a snuggly teddy kitty—chubby and squeezably unfit, and in no way a coyote-fighting warrior cat-machine.

I took off running through the forest in the direction of the shrieking, Joe at my heels, as we scrambled to try to save Tuna from the coyote. Joe caught a glimpse of the coyote through the trees, but there was no way we could ever catch him. We heard more screaming and fighting, and I had a very visible breakdown, knowing my cat was gone; he had no chance against that.

I was bawling and sobbing, flailing and wailing. It was all my fault my cat was dead because I hadn't watched him close enough, and the thought of him dying in such a horrific way destroyed me. Joe had to physically prop me up as we inched our way out of the woods and slowly stumbled back toward the house.

Joe was at a loss as to how to comfort me; I was inconsolable. He'd never seen me so out of control, so desolate, and he just kept me upright and moving in the right direction.

As we neared the house, passing the shed at the top of the slope, Joe pointed at our front porch. "Look, honey," he said gently. "Tuna's sitting right there."

No! I couldn't believe my eyes! It was too good to be true!

It couldn't be true. I refused to believe it at first. I'd heard my cat dying.

But…there he was. It was Tuna, sitting on the front porch watching us, not a care in the world, and looking at me like I'd lost my damned mind.

Well. This was awkward.

What did I do or say to my husband now after the scene I'd just made? *"Oh, my bad. Sorry about that incredibly insane breakdown you were just forced to witness. Let us never speak of this again."*

I had just spent the last half hour chasing a coyote through the woods and full-out mourning the very cat who now eyed me suspiciously, wondering what all the hubbub was about and why I'd inconvenienced him by not letting him inside the house when he'd knocked.

"Tuna, you can't ever die," said Joe, shaking his head slowly, laughing nervously, and giving me the freaked-out side-eye. "I can't go through that ever again."

I agreed.

Let us never repeat that experience.

And never tell a soul what occurred here.

Except for you, dear reader.

You can keep a secret, right?

I picked up Una, cradled him in my arms, kissed his squishy face until he told me to "talk to the paw", and have squeezed him gently every day since, pretending there will never come a day where it's not a Trial Run.

☙❧

I remember that snot-nosed kitten that I wished I didn't have to deal with. And Mary, whose burdens I never wanted to make my own.

Today, I'm so, so glad that I did.

Because isn't that the true beauty of rescue?

The chance at encountering a love so fierce you feel you cannot go on after its leaving?

Animal rescuers know that love doesn't confine itself only to the bounds of humanity; it readily breaks the chains of separation and wraps itself around all of earth's creatures.

I wouldn't have it any other way.

☙❧

Tamira Thayne is the author of *The Wrath of Dog, The King's Tether, Foster Doggie Insanity,* and *Capitol in Chains,* and the co-editor of *Unchain My Heart* and *Rescue Smiles.*

Tamira pioneered the anti-tethering movement in America, forming and leading the nonprofit Dogs Deserve Better for 13 years; her swan song culminated in the purchase and transformation of Michael Vick's dogfighting compound to a chained-dog rescue and rehabilitation center.

HOME AT LAST:
Sarge

BY REG GREEN

I'VE SPENT MOST OF MY LIFE, with the exception of my college years, living in the suburbs of Chicago. Therefore, it was no small adjustment for me to pick up and move 100 miles south of Chicago, into east central Illinois, following my retirement from a teaching career that I considered one of my greatest blessings.

My wife Beckie and I purchased a home on a beautiful private lake, nestled—quite hidden—within a copse of mature woods surrounded by small rural towns and an abundance of beautiful fertile farmlands. It was our own "On Golden Pond."

We very soon found an abundance of friendliness and acceptance towards newcomers and strangers here, which I found a bit different at first. People waved to me from their cars when I passed them on a country road like we talked every day, even though we'd never been introduced to each other in person.

It was just humanity greeting humanity, which was nice, and I quickly grew to enjoy it, because, that's just what we do down here. This was a far cry from what I'd been used to, living in the "hurry up" world of the Chicago area for so long.

There are only two options when you want to make the drive into our little town five miles away to do shopping of any kind. You either take what we called "the lake road" or you take "the back road". I found myself splitting my time equally between both of these options; after all, I had to see who I might pass and receive a wave from.

After several years at our new residence, I was adjusting to our new lifestyle and feeling quite comfortable. Having now made some very good friends and become active in various community and church affairs, I was convinced that this was indeed the retirement life that we all dream of.

I was still able to pick up my old Chicago radio stations quite well in the car, and I'd be lying if I told you I didn't chuckle to myself when I would hear traffic reports describing stop-and-go traffic and five-mile back-ups on a particular expressway I knew all too well. All the while, I was traveling at my leisurely pace, past rows of corn and soybeans while going from town to town.

I found that when you travel in rural areas a lot and the landscape scenery changes in any way you tend to notice.

Even the smallest additions can make a huge difference in your memory from other trips taken along the same route. Along our lake road I had recently noticed a large black dog sitting in a yard watching traffic go by. He was probably a lab or lab mix of some kind. Being a dog lover, I found myself sitting up and taking notice, now, and even driving that way deliberately to see if the dog was still there.

On subsequent trips, I noticed that the black dog was chained to a large tree in a yard, probably several hundred feet from the rural residence. There was an older doghouse sitting in the shade below the tree. It always seemed to me that when I passed the dog on the chain, he or she would follow me with what seemed to be sad, pleading eyes.

For all I knew the dog followed every passing car the same way, but I began to convince myself that he only followed me that way. I also tried to convince myself that the dog was probably being brought into the house every night to join the family. However, my intellect was telling me that I doubted this was really happening—because this dog was ALWAYS out there on the chain.

Was it a coincidence that he just happened to be chained when I passed by? I could not come to convince myself of that.

I can't remember exactly under what circumstances, but I later learned that the dog's name was Sarge. It might have been one of my many breakfasts with the guys at the local coffee shop, but I was glad that I could now think of and refer to him by name.

That added, at the very least, a little dignity to the living being I was beginning to feel a great degree of empathy for. What must life be like for him—perpetually chained? Days passed to weeks. Weeks became months . . . and then silently years—while Sarge remained ever chained.

Passing by Sarge became a daily duty for me by now. I had to at least do that for the guy who was so often on my mind throughout the day, and even made regular appearances in my nightly dreams.

I do admit to occasionally, under cover of darkness, parking my car across the street from Sarge's residence and quietly walking over to him to deliver cheeseburgers from a local restaurant—which in my opinion, was the very least he deserved.

On one occasion I actually took his chain in my hand to see how heavy it was, and could not help but wonder if it might have sufficed at holding a naval destroyer at port. Its weight and thickness was far beyond what was needed for its current purpose.

That next winter was almost beyond my comprehension in terms of cruel weather. Words like "bitter" and "bone chilling" came nowhere near to accurately describing what our area was going through. I couldn't even imagine what Sarge was enduring, but the thought of him stuck outdoors in the weather haunted me.

On January 4th of that year the temperature was 9 degrees below zero with a wind chill of 25 degrees below zero. We had just accumulated over a foot of snow, and there sat Sarge on the frozen ice and mud around his doghouse staring at me as I drove by.

Of course, he knew my car by now.

I was very worried that he might not survive much longer in the severe conditions. Desperate for any idea, I called our county sheriff department, hoping and praying that someone there could give me some instruction and point me in a direction get Sarge out of harm's way. The dispatcher asked me several questions. One question was in regards to the availability of water. Water?!

How could there be any water when the outside temperature is nine degrees below zero, I thought. When I was asked if the dog was within our city limits I began to reply "Well, just barely…he's…." and then I was cut off.

"Then there's nothing we can do," I was told. "You have to call your mayor." I thanked the dispatcher—not really sure what I was thanking him for since he'd been zero help—but I had been taught to end most calls this way, I guess.

My next call was to our mayor, whom I knew. When I told him that the sheriff's office had instructed me to call him regarding the situation, his only response was, "What am I supposed to do about it?" By this point it was becoming quite clear to me that absolutely nothing was going to happen here, legally or illegally, unless I did it myself.

By now I was having trouble sleeping. The next day the temperature had dipped another degree to 10 below zero. The winds were howling. What was now a daily drive-by to see if Sarge had survived the night before had become a fear-filled and obsessive mission.

On the morning of January 5th, I really was not sure I would see a living dog when I drove by. I didn't know how he could have survived a night of such frigid temperatures. I was beside myself with anxiety, but I finally saw a black figure in the doghouse, head peering out. As I watched for movement, I saw none for what seemed like hours. *Please move Sarge…please just move a little,* I thought. *Show me you have not frozen to death overnight.*

Then, finally, I saw some tiny movement. Sarge did not or could not venture out of his house, but he was alive. That's all I knew for sure.

As I was driving back home an idea came to me. Just a few weeks ago I had spearheaded our parish Christmas party at my church. I still had a few sheets left over of the festive Christmas letterhead I had purchased for the invitations. I grabbed a piece and began to write a note to Sarge's owner.

In the note, I very politely offered to take Sarge in through the worst of the treacherous, brutal cold spell we were going through and offered to bring him back when the weather broke and conditions improved. I left my cell phone number and signed my name. There was nobody at home, so I left the note in an envelope inside the outer door. I left, and hoped for the best.

The next day, January 6th, the temperature had dropped 2 more degrees to 12 below zero. The radio reported that wind chills were now at 31 degrees below zero. I swear I was actually feeling Sarge's discomfort, even though I was warm and cozy in my home. Apparently, that is what this empathy thing is all about. And it hurt.

Again, I drove past the home. I saw something black in the doghouse, but again no movement. I was scared and frantic. I continued just a bit down the road. I didn't know what to do, but I knew I had to do something.

As I began to turn around to go back, my cell phone rang. I pulled the car over and parked it. I didn't recognize the number. Could this be Sarge's owner? What was I about to hear? A "mind your own business" scolding?

"Hello, is this Reg?" a male voice asked.

"Yes, this is Reg."

A pause…which seemed to go on for an eternity.

"Reg, I'm going to take you up on your offer to take Sarge." The man said. I gasped when he continued: " In fact, you can have Sarge. I can no longer take care of him."

Stunned beyond belief, I stammered out a thank you.

I said I would be by very soon to get him, not knowing yet if there was any life left to save. But for the first time in a long time, I felt excited and hopeful.

I called my good friend, Tom, who knew all about Sarge. I said "Tom, Sarge was just surrendered to me. Will you meet me over there with your van in 10 minutes to help me get him?"

Tom was as excited as I was. I went home to change into warmer clothes, and quickly returned to Sarge's home, where I found Tom already parked outside.

We both got out and walked toward Sarge. He was still alive! He stepped out of his house and just sat on the snow and ice, not moving or showing any emotion. We rushed to him, anxious to get him out of the cold, only to discover that the lock on his chain was frozen shut! We tried every tool we'd carried with us, including WD-40, but had no luck.

We finally decided to just cut his collar off and let it fall to the ground. It was cathartic for me, symbolic of us freeing him from this chain. We fastened a leash and a brand new collar on him, and we again made our way through the snowdrifts back to the van. Neither Tom nor I was yet capable of driving the car, because we were so cold and numbness had set into our hands. How did this poor dog survive this frigid weather for days on end?

I didn't have an answer, but I was just so grateful that he had.

The three of us sat quietly together in the warm van.

I had already made a phone call to my local veterinarian clinic telling them that Sarge had been surrendered to me, and I would be bringing him into the clinic in just a few minutes for a full check-up and exam.

"You have Sarge?" the wonderful receptionist at the vet clinic asked.

"Yes I have Sarge." I smiled. Everyone knew about Sarge, and what his life had been like out there on that chain. And now there was genuine interest from so many to learn more about him.

"Just bring him directly back to the exam room, Reg. We'll be ready for you."

Boy, was that good to hear! Still not knowing anything about his health in light of all he'd been through, we headed for the clinic, which was about 15 minutes away. Tom and I had both noticed that there was no evidence of any food or water for Sarge when we had arrived. We made a decision to stop at the local hamburger shop in town, and I bought four cheeseburgers for Sarge.

With Tom driving to the clinic, I carefully unwrapped each cheeseburger and gently offered it to Sarge. The poor boy swooped in immediately and almost swallowed the first one whole. I suggested he chew them, but he was too excited.

The veterinarian began the difficult task of examining Sarge, without any information about the dog's medical history. We didn't know his age, shot history, anything. At one point in the exam he admitted Sarge might not have made it through another night outside in the brutally cold weather.

Sarge sat like a gentleman during the very thorough exam.

After the vet had finished I asked if I might leave Sarge there with him for a few days for observation, and to get him started on some good nutrition habits. His urine had been a very bright yellow, which was an indicator of probable dehydration. He agreed, and I felt so relieved to be leaving him in such capable, knowledgable hands. I learned that my veterinarian had made his best guess estimate as to Sarge's age, and thought him to be around nine years old.

Word had traveled quickly around our lake community that I was now Sarge's new owner. I learned that dozens and dozens of people had been passing by Sarge over the years and feeling anguish and helplessness for the big guy, too. Word on the street was that Reg had "rescued" Sarge.

I very nicely asked people not to use the word rescue as that seemed to put the emphasis more on me than on him. Sarge was the hero to have survived the conditions that he did, for as long as he had.

As an example of the heart and compassion of our community, I ended up receiving five different $100.00 donations for his veterinary care and follow up. In the days after his freedom from the chain, my intention was to look for a wonderful adoptive family for him that would give him everything—and I mean everything—that he had never had the chance to enjoy about humanity and life in general.

Yes, that was the plan—at the time.

I took out display ads in three central Illinois newspapers seeking adopters for Sarge. The ads all read the same in large bold letters: "Nine-year-old black lab with a story that will bring you to tears needs the greatest home. Serious inquiries only please." And I left both my home and cell numbers.

I ran the ads for three consecutive weeks, through the end

of January. After three weeks, and having received no calls whatsoever, I pulled the ads. It had been costly venture on my part that produced no results. Now what?

With Sarge still being cared for at the veterinary clinic, and the bills really starting to add up, I approached my wife Beckie with great hesitation and sheepishly asked if I might bring Sarge back to our home for awhile—at least to stop the bill from climbing on Sarge's boarding. With a bit of hesitation she agreed.

We already had a nine-year-old female Cocker spaniel living with us, and immediately we both began to question how compatible the two would be in our home. There was no other way to learn the answer to this query, though, than to make it happen and find out.

I went to get Sarge and brought him home. After mutually sniffing each other all over, they both decided they'd honestly rather sniff other things. To actually be in a house, a home, a dwelling—where humans lived—was something so new for Sarge that he appeared to be in complete awe of everything.

One thing that became immediately obvious to both Beckie and me was that Sarge was not leaving my side. Not under any circumstances. Where I went, he was going also.

It was after the third or fourth day of having Sarge with us that I took a huge chance. I asked Beckie if maybe, just maybe, we could keep him and stop the search for an adoptive family.

When she agreed—without much hesitation, mind you— my heart was full, and I was beyond pleased to know I'd acquired a new best friend. It seemed like the right and perfect ending to my quest for Sarge's freedom.

The likes of our bonding, after three years and counting,

I will most likely never see again. To this day Sarge still does not leave my side, going everywhere with me. And while many no doubt might find this annoying, I consider it a blessing. I was not aware that I had the capacity to love and care for another being the way I do for Sarge.

I vividly remember one night in Sarge's first week at our home experiencing a significant rainstorm. Thunder boomed, and lightning streaked past our windows. After the first blast, I found a 70-pound mass of shivering dog climbing onto my lap on the couch of my office.

The poor guy was trembling so badly! I held him tight and continued to talk to him while petting him and rubbing his fur all over. All the while, I was wondering what it must have been like for him to experience nighttime thunderstorms while chained to a tree for so many years of his life.

I was determined that he would never have to experience trauma like that again. He was the hero. It wasn't me, to be sure. And as I finish writing his story, I want you to know that Sarge is still sitting only about 3" from my right leg. I believe he thanks me every day of his life for getting him out of that situation in the only way he knows how: by loyally staying by my side.

I know that there will be readers who question why I did not confront Sarge's owner much sooner than I did…why I let him suffer for so long. I can't give you a definitive answer other than to say I am not, and have never been about, confrontation.

To this day I do not speak badly about his previous owner, because I know he did the right thing in the end. And in so doing gave me one of the best gifts I've ever been given, though at the time I couldn't know that.

For now, I'm comforted in knowing he's My Sarge.

Authors note: For the record, after years of sleeping in an old leaky doghouse and laying on frozen mud and snow, Sarge now sleeps on a queen-sized bed with flannel sheets and (my) pillows. He's earned it far more than I ever have.

๖ؤ

Reg Green is a retired high school teacher and coach from the Chicago suburbs. Since his retirement from education 10 years ago, he has self published two dog books as fundraisers for various dog rescue organizations around the U.S., with 100% of sales proceeds going right back to the rescues themselves. He has designed tee shirts for rescue organizations to use in sales and promotion, along with posters advocating for dog welfare—especially anti-chaining posters on behalf of the perpetually chained dog. He does some public speaking in central Illinois libraries and to civic groups on "Our Gift of Dogs." He has attended conferences around the U.S. advocating for more humane treatment for our animal friends. And as Reg puts it—he has completely "Gone to the Dogs" since retiring.

HEART OF A RAT:
Sabre

BY HEATHER LEUGHMYER

RAT: A CRINGE-WORTHY WORD to so many who are brought up with the expectations that these "vermin" merely live in sewers and carry disease. After all, weren't those the nasty little creatures responsible for the Bubonic Plague? (In actuality, it was the fleas who hitched a ride on the rats who spread the disease.) Rats have gotten a bad rap that they definitely don't deserve. Thanks to the melodrama of Hollywood and the media, the majority of people don't understand rats, nor do they want to; what we don't understand often unjustifiably terrifies us.

Yes, rats enjoy scavenging, and human trash can be

immensely tasty. Rats are foodies, after all—as many of us can relate to—and they will definitely take advantage of the scrumptious delicacies that we throw away. But the truth is rats are basically just squirrels with naked tails. If we don't want them in our lives, there are precautions we can and should take to make our environments less appealing to them.

But these, of course, are the wild variety. What most folks don't know is that domestic rats are as much like their wild cousins as domestic dogs are to wolves. Much like dogs, companion rats are intelligent, affectionate and personable.

"Not under my roof," I was told each time I pleaded for a pet rat as a teen. When I finally got out from under that roof, the first thing I did was run to the nearest pet shop with one thing on my mind: my rat! There I chose a "large" black and white hooded rat from a crowded 10-gallon tank labeled "pet or feeder."

Most likely he would have ended up in some snake's belly had I not come across him when I did. After telepathically telling the others I was sorry I couldn't take them all, I scooped him up, took him to his new home, and named him Sabre. Little did I know that my pocket-sized friend and his antics would forever change my life.

Sabre and I immediately bonded. He seemed to know that I had saved him from some unfortunate fate, and I could actually sense how extremely grateful he was. He quickly became accustomed to burrowing inside my sweatshirt where he would kiss and groom me while bruxing and boggling (the rat version of purring).

I had crafted a large cage for him, but apparently my crafting skills were lacking because he became an expert at breaking out whenever his little heart desired. Eventually I gave up and just let him sleep where he wanted to sleep, which just so happened to be my bed. Due to his habit of creating cozy nests from the stuffing of my comforter I went through several of them before eventually giving up. He was worth it.

Sabre was a social butterfly. I was in college and friends would come and go on a regular basis. When he heard the voice of someone new he would hop eagerly across the floor and leap onto their laps. Some loved him, some didn't, but he never failed to entertain. He was smart. He knew his name and responded better to it than most cats or dogs I have known. I taught him tricks with treats and he was always the hit of any party. Lucky for him, college kids like pizza because so do rats, and he savored every bite. Most people, after they got to know him, couldn't help but adore him. He was my baby boy. My heart-rat. My soulmate. And I never doubted for a second that he felt the same about me.

Sabre and I cohabitated like this for three wonderful years. Him, scampering through the house, cuddling with me in bed, sharing my dinner, entertaining guests, living life to the fullest, and just basically being completely lovable; me, enjoying his company as often as possible, smiling and laughing, while sadly understanding that his time with me was very limited. It was bittersweet.

Somewhere around my junior year his body began to shut down. I awoke one morning to see him struggling so I skipped class and lay with him in bed until we both fell asleep. When I woke up, his soul had left his body, but his tiny hand was still gripping tightly to my sweatshirt like one last "I love you."

My heart was shattered. I buried him in the yard and planted a sapling over his grave.

Sabre left an imprint on my soul that I could never really put into words. He was not only my best friend, but my teacher. Among other lessons, he taught me that size and species are irrelevant when it comes to giving and receiving love. He also opened my eyes to the cruelties involved in the pet trade.

I've matured a lot since Sabre was a part of my life. I stopped supporting pet shops and breeders and founded Happy Endings Rat Rescue. I began rescuing, rehabilitating and rehoming domestic rats and mice. Since the rescue was founded, hundreds of rats and other small animals have passed through my hands, or stayed here to live out their lives in sanctuary. Over the years I have had the pleasure of getting to know many delightful and unique rattie personalities, and I have loved each and every one of them.

My heart will forever hold a place for these overlooked and misunderstood little earthlings. As long as I am alive and capable, I will continue to do what I can to not only rescue as many as possible, but to educate others about these precious individuals while continuing to shatter negative stereotypes.

Rest in Peace Sabre and all those who have followed. I'll never forget you. This poem is dedicated to all those I have loved and lost and to the billions more who suffer at the hands of humans:

Rat

Vilified by Hollywood
Blamed for a disease
That dark, consuming shadow crept
Not from you, but from your fleas
You suffer undefended
At the mercy of men in white
Drugged, deprived, shocked, and sliced
Yet rarely do you bite.

Expendably inexpensive
To those easily seduced
By carnivorous constrictors
You're recklessly reproduced
Provisions for ball pythons
Uncomplicated prey
Confined inside four walls of glass
Victim of the day.

Your bodies are broken
With the sharp snap of steel
You writhe with convulsions
From a poisoned meal
Slow death by starvation
Immobilized in glue
A living being so despised
Just because you're you.

Your willowy whiskers vibrate
Teeth grinding like a purr
Your eyes contented little slits
As I caress your fur
Overflowing with affection
This guiltless little creature
To some may seem a curse
To those who love, a teacher.

⟡

Heather Leughmyer is the author of *Adopting Adele, Brave Benny, A Rat's Guide to Owning a Human*, and *If Your Tears Were Human*, and co-editor of *Rescue Smiles*. She is also the founder of Happy Endings Rat Rescue, and a graduate of Indiana-Purdue University with a B.A. in Writing and Linguistics.

Writing has been a passion of hers for as long as she has advocated for animals.

She lives in Columbia City, Indiana, with her husband, daughter, and several animal companions.

IN THE BEGINNING:
Blue and Ranger

BY JOE MARINGO

THE NUMBER OF BEAUTIFUL DOGS that have come through my doors in the past 17 years still amazes me. I would never have believed way back then, while working as an outdoor guide in very rural Texas, that one skinny stray dog would start something so meaningful. But that's how the Southwest Pennsylvania Retriever Rescue Organization (also known as SPARRO) story began, as something innocuous that later bears fruit, the path becoming obvious only in hindsight. I had no idea at the time that it would blossom into something so rich and purposeful for me.

That horribly neglected dog was a young bluetick hound that came wandering into the yard of our camp while I was cleaning up after a long day. He sat and watched me, unmoving, his sad eyes following my every move. Having dogs of my own at home in Pennsylvania, I couldn't stand to see him in such poor condition, so I threw him some scraps, knowing he had to be starving. He politely picked them up and slowly wandered away.

I figured that would be the last I saw of him, but 20 minutes later he was back, laying in his spot and quietly keeping me in his sight. I walked over to pet him, and he cringed away as I reached out to touch him. It was obvious that he had not had the best interactions with humans. Still, he stayed and let me pet him while I spoke softly and quietly to him.

Since he was a bluetick hound, it seemed like a no brainer to me to name him Blue, so that's what I started calling him. Although he was a bit shy, he was still sweet as could be. I spent 10 or 15 minutes petting and talking to him, and then had to get back to finishing my day's work. By then it was nearing 10:00 p.m., and I just wanted to be done with it. I tossed him another round of scraps, and he wandered off again while I finished up for the night.

I normally worked in Texas for about two weeks, and then drove back to Pennsylvania for a week to take care of things at home, and I briefly wondered if I'd ever see him again. I sent some good thoughts his way as I left for Pennsylvania the next morning.

I didn't see him again for several weeks. I had been back in Texas for over a week when he came wandering into the yard where we were all just sitting around and having an evening drink. I spied him in the shadows and called to him, "c'meer Blue!" The neighbors were not happy to hear me encouraging him and asked why I wanted that mangy mutt around. I told them he was a nice dog and asked if they knew who owned him or if they knew anything about him.

"Oh, he's just another stray; there are hundreds of them round these parts." Seems Blue had been running around for a month or more, getting into people's trash and doing the things a stray does in order to survive. I asked what would become of him and was shocked to hear he was already slated to be shot on sight by several people for tearing up their garbage. At that point someone threw something in his direction and he took off running, justifiably scared. It was obvious to me that this had happened to him more than a few times before. I was disturbed.

It was three more days until I saw Blue again. Once again I was working around the camp, and once again he just sat and watched, only this time he wagged his tail when I spoke to him. I walked over to him and he let me pet him without any fear. I guess he knew I had become kind of fond of him. I gave him some food and sat with him for quite awhile, and finally said these words to him that I will never forget. "Blue, if you're here on Friday when I head for home, I'll take you with me."

That was on a Tuesday evening. He promptly stood up, turned, and trotted off into the darkness. I didn't see him again the rest of the week, and I feared that someone had collected the bounty on his head. I thought of him often throughout the day, and it made me sad to think he might be gone. Friday morning at 5:00 a.m. I woke with the sunrise, finished packing, and was all set to make the long 1200 mile trip home. I closed everything down in the cabin and headed for the truck.

To my surprise, laying on the front porch fast asleep was Blue, and he had another surprise waiting for me—the cutest little black and white puppy, only eight or ten weeks old. Blue slowly picked his head up in that sweet, slow, houndy way and looked at me with those sad hound eyes. "Well, I guess you're telling me you want to bring your friend along to Pennsylvania with you, huh?" They both stood up and wagged their entire bodies.

That was it, the decision was made; two dogs were going back with me, and I would figure out what to do with them when I got home.

The little guy needed a good Texas name. Because he was just out wandering the range, and because their baseball team was named the Rangers, that would quickly become his name. Blue and Ranger were southern boys being transplanted into Yankee country. At least we would treat them right and give them a great life up north.

As the boys had been living in the bush, they were both covered with hundreds of ticks and thousands of fleas. Luckily, there was a small country veterinarian's office just one town over in Haskell, Texas. Roseann, the vet tech, was so thrilled that I was helping these two that she bathed them, treated them for their parasites both inside and out, vaccinated them, and didn't charge me a penny. She was a nice lady and it was the first time in my life I felt like I was doing something special and someone else thought so too.

The boys were clean, vaccinated and ready to head north, except for one thing I'd forgotten—all the nasty stuff the two had been eating since God knows when. At first it was the gas that almost drove me out of the truck, but I just put the windows down a little more, resolving to just get through it.

Then I suddenly realized that it was more than just gas I was smelling—yep, you guessed it.

I stopped every ten miles for the first hour or so to clean up accidents and places where one or the other had thrown up. This became my first and one of my most valuable rescue lessons: transport rescue dogs on an empty stomach! The rest of the trip was uneventful. I normally drove straight through, and, desperate to get these guys home and into shape for adoption, that was what I did this time, too.

Nineteen hours later we'd reached my home, and now I had to figure out what to do with two dogs I knew nothing about. I didn't even know if they would get along with my own dogs, and I worried that the parasites they had would spread to my guys. So I set up a room in my basement as a quarantine area and got them all settled in for the night.

This is when I learned rescue lesson number two: always expect the unexpected! It just so happened that that night was a beautiful, clear night in Pennsylvania, with a huge, full moon. The dogs had only been in their room for a few minutes when the howling started. Low at first and then louder and louder, until I was sure every window in the neighborhood was rattling from the sound. I knew this wouldn't work and I would have to do something about it.

I reluctantly got out of bed and went outside and around to the basement, just in time to hear Blue break the glass in the window of his room. I was sure he'd mortally injured himself, but he didn't have a scratch on him. I threw up a quick sheet of plywood over the window, which would have to work for the night; it came with the added bonus that he would not be able to see the moon. There was a little howling and barking throughout the night, but it wasn't as bad as before. We all got some much-needed sleep and were up and working on their training bright and early the next morning.

Blue and Ranger were a great pair. They played together like littermates and loved running in the fenced yard. I was elated at how well they behaved, and was even happier that they got along with my own dogs. After a few days of allowing their bodies to clear of all the nasty stuff inside and out, they got to start interacting with all of my guys. I had thought at first I would keep Blue, but knew I had to find a home for Ranger, as he was young and rambunctious—plus, he was highly adoptable.

I posted fliers, ran ads in the newspaper, and told everyone I knew about the sweet little pup. It was not until the first family came to visit that I heard those words everyone in rescue eventually hears, "oh, I don't think we're interested because he is a pit puppy." We had always had mutts growing up, and I just figured him for a mutt. That took me by surprise, and I realized there were so many things I didn't yet know about this adventure called dog rescue.

Looking back now, I can see that he was the poster pup for the pit breed. I don't fault him for it, and actually love the breed for the most part; we have rescued dozens of pits and pit mixes over the years. Ranger had several other families come visit him, and they all said the same thing. I began to wonder if we would ever find him a home.

I also started to wonder if we were the right family for Blue. He was happy with us and doing well, but I could tell he wanted more. He needed a family that was more active and took him out to run in the woods. As it ended up, the decision would be made for me quite easily.

About a week later, a very nice lady contacted me to come

meet Ranger. I could tell right away she was smitten with him, and being a pitty puppy, Ranger just loved everyone. She had come with her sister, and while she played with Ranger her sister asked me what the deal was with Blue so I filled her in on his story. She said she really loved his color and he seemed like a nice dog. After getting some background information on her, I made the choice to put Blue up for adoption. She said she would have to talk to her family, but really thought she would like to adopt him.

Sometimes that's just how things work in rescue; no interest in anyone for weeks, and then all of a sudden two get adopted in one day. It was the perfect adoption because the sisters live next door to each other, and the dogs could visit whenever they wanted. They would have their own families, but still have each other. The next weekend everything was finalized. Contracts were signed and the adoption was done. I was so happy for both dogs, but in the back of my mind I missed them and wondered what I had just experienced. I had never heard of pet rescue at that time, and did not even know anything like that existed. I did decide though, that I might just try to bring a dog back with me on every trip home from Texas. It didn't seem too difficult, and it would make a huge difference in the dogs' lives.

There have been many dogs since those first two, and many new lessons to learn along the way. Unfortunately, Blue did not work out with his family, and he came back to me some time later. It was not that bad though; he was re-adopted soon and went to live with a very nice computer software company owner. Blue lived the life of a king there, and went to work with his "dad" every day.

In an update he told me it was Blue's job to walk around

to every desk at least two or three times and day for ear rubs and a treat. It was a job he took very seriously. He even got the nickname "Mayor of Washington" because of his good will and loving nature. Blue even became a hero when the office building his dad worked in caught on fire. I will never forget the news footage from the helicopter of Blue running back and forth across the roof of the Washington Hotel making sure all his friends and coworkers got out safely.

They all did, and so did Blue. I lost track of him after that, and since it has been 17 years since his rescue, I am sad to think he has probably passed. I bet he is sitting at the base of the Rainbow Bridge right now and howling at the full moon there.

Ranger is a different story. He stayed with his original family his entire life. Again, I lost track of him after a few years, but I often thought of them both fondly. I now go to our local Monroeville, Pennsylvania Petco every Sunday morning for meet and greets with a rescue dog or two. A little over a year ago a nice family walked up to me with a senior dog. They looked, and smiled, and ask me if I knew who they were. I have to be honest; those years have been hard on me as well.

I used to remember faces really well, and I always remembered the dogs, but my memory is not what it used to be. I was a bit embarrassed when I told them that sadly, I did not think I remembered them. As soon as they told me that the dog's name was Ranger my eyes filled with tears. I was amazed he was still around and was doing pretty well. I sat on the floor with him for a long time, and we talked about all that had happened in the past 16 years. Awhile later, it was time for them to go. I got a picture of my pitty boy before they left, though. I still think about him quite often and hope he is still with us; but if not, I know he is right next to Blue at the bridge, where they roll and play and wait for us to come find them again.

⟬⟭

Joe Maringo is the Director of Southwest Pennsylvania Retriever Rescue Org/S.P.A.R.R.O. and Shades of Grey Sanctuary For Senior Dogs in Plum, Pennsylvania. Over the years SPARRO has grown and to date they have rescued over 1,000 dogs, from every single state east of the Rockies and from Canada as well. Donate for their rescue efforts at www. sparro.org.

COMING IN FROM THE COLD:
Misty

BY PATTI LAWSON

I REFUSED TO MOVE WITH MY FAMILY to Pennsylvania from Arizona until my Dad promised to buy me a pony. The thought of my very own pony propelled me to help pack, say goodbye to my friends, and endure the long drive across the country to where I envisioned my beautiful pony was waiting for me in a hay-infused barn.

Instead we arrived at a former chicken farm in the middle of the night, Dad cheerfully shining a flashlight on a dark and looming structure and informing me that was where my pony would live. I was beginning to think this didn't look very promising, but Dad was so joyful about our new home as he lugged all the sleeping bags into this strange house, that I didn't have the heart to make a fuss.

It took a lot of work that summer to make the former chicken farm into our home. Every day I questioned Dad as to when my pony would be arriving, and every day he promised "soon." By the time fall arrived all the old chicken pens had been torn down, and the old farmhouse was starting to feel like a real home.

I had chosen a place in the barn for my future pony and cleaned it out, looking at it hopefully each morning. That it remained empty was troublesome to me, and before I'd get on the school bus I always asked if my pony would be there when I got home.

Dad's answer was always the same. "We'll see."

Our first cold Pennsylvania winter arrived, and we weren't prepared. The wind howled at night and rattled the windows of our old house. I longed for Arizona, the sunshine, and my friends. I prayed for my pony every night, but I quit asking because I had given up hope.

Then one very frigid night when my Dad got home from work he took a wrinkled piece of paper out of his lunchbox and excitedly smoothed it out on the table. It was a notice that a pony farm not far away was closing and they needed homes for the remaining ponies. My Dad said he would borrow a truck from a friend and we would go get my pony on Saturday.

I could hardly believe it! I dreamed of her every night for the rest of the week, and the days and hours could not tick by fast enough to bring me to the weekend and my very own pony.

Dad ended up having to work on Saturday, and I was so disappointed I cried. I moped around all day—angry, sad, and wondering if I could possibly run off to Arizona where I could live with my friend Becky. I was deep in thought at this glimmer of hope when Dad got home, yelling "Let's go," as he burst through the door.

My brother Bill and I grabbed our boots and jackets and ran out to jump in the truck my dad had borrowed. The pony farm turned out to be a big disappointment. Ragged horses were barely visible standing in the corral outside the barn; they were silent and still in the freezing air. Dad talked to the owner as my brother and I stood quietly, waiting.

We were afraid of the large shapes whose breath you could see wafting in the moonlight.

My dad told us that we could each pick a pony and we walked slowly through the pack, looking them over. He told us these ponies needed us, and that we would give them a good home so they wouldn't go hungry any more. He showed us how to approach them gently and touch them softly. They had ice frozen on their fur and were quiet and sad.

I had read Marguerite Henry's book, *Misty of Chincoteague,* over and over until I had worn it out and had to tape the pages. That night, in that dark ramshackle barn, I found my Misty. She looked just like the pony in the book, and was standing next to a slightly larger pony, both brown and white pintos. She nudged me with her soft nose as I gently stroked her neck which was covered in little frozen ice balls. There was no question; I'd found my pony.

My dad talked to the owner and soon Misty (I had already named her) and the larger pony were secure in the truck and we were on our way home. We unloaded them at the barn and put them in stalls next to each other. In the big overhead light, they looked so skinny and defeated, standing with their heads hanging down.

Dad put old army blankets on them and tied them with rope. He said they needed to warm up and this would help melt the ice on their fur. We added more straw to their stalls for extra warmth, too. They ate the hay hungrily, and my dad gave them each a big scoop of oats. I wanted to stay in the barn, but Dad said I could come out first thing in the morning. We reluctantly shut out the lights and left them to ponder their new home.

The rest of that winter, we eagerly cared for our ponies and watched as they changed and grew healthier. The ice was soon off their fur, and we were able to start brushing them daily. I spent hours after school and on the weekends talking to and bonding with Misty. She was everything I'd ever hoped for and more.

My brother named his pony Marble because she bore the same swirling colors as one of his marbles. Both ponies gained weight during the winter, and when spring came they were beautiful, healthy, and happily settled into their new home.

One spring morning my brother and I noticed a large brown "something" next to Marble in the pasture. At first we thought it was a stray dog, or maybe even a deer. As we got closer it stood and it was a beautiful reddish chestnut colt! We screamed and ran to the house to get Dad.

It turned out that Marble had not just been gaining weight from the food—she had been pregnant when we brought her home, but due to her poor condition, no one had even noticed.

Misty became my best friend during my high school years and beyond. Through training Misty, I learned to challenge myself as I challenged her. I taught her barrel racing, jumping over low hurdles, walking sideways, bowing down, and other tricks.

I rode her the three miles to our little country store when I had enough money for a Pepsi, which I would always share with her. I often took a peanut butter sandwich, a book, and Misty, and we would escape my very noisy house (I had six brothers and sisters). Misty and I would wander the countryside for hours, finally finding a spot where I'd hook a rope to my ankle, lay down on the grass to read, and share my sandwich with Misty.

I trudged through four-foot snowdrifts to get to the barn to feed and water her in the winter, and pulled endless buckets of water up from the well to fill her water trough during the hot summer months. Our bond grew and cemented even into my college years as I continued to love and care for her.

One night, while I was working as a desk clerk at a local hotel, the door to the lobby opened and it was my dad. He had never come there before so I braced myself, fearing something bad had happened to someone in the family. I stepped out from behind the desk and sat down on the sofa beside him.

He put his arms around me, and told me that my sweet Misty had died. I knew she was quite old by now, but in truth I had never contemplated her death. Dad held me as I sobbed. He said tomorrow we would bury Misty down by the pine grove where she loved to run.

He held true to his word, and we buried Misty in her

favorite spot the next day. I placed her brush, halter, bridle, and blanket in the grave with her. On top, I laid my tattered copy of the book that she was named for.

I sat there for a long time after my dad left. Finally, I trudged up the hill to the house, knowing that my life would always have an empty space without her, but also knowing I'd given my beautiful pony my very best in our countless happy hours together. I had to move forward without her.

Thoughts of Misty have stayed with me all these years, and the connection of our souls continues to inspire me to this day.

ॐ

Patti Lawson is an award-winning author, lawyer, newspaper columnist and public speaker who lives in West Virginia, with her dogs Sadie and Rusty. Patti's first book, *The Dog Diet, A Memoir: What My Dog Taught Me About Shedding Pounds, Licking Stress and Getting a new Leash on Life* (HCI, Publishing, Inc., 2006) won the Dog Writer's Association of America Maxwell Award for Dog Humor Book. *The Dog Diet* was also honored by being listed on the McNaughton Library List. She is a frequent contributor to The Huffington Post and AOL Paw Nation.

Patti's love of the law and dogs came together in her new book *What Happens to Rover When the Marriage is Over, and Other Doggone Legal Dilemmas!* (Skyhorse Publishing, September, 2016). Rover won the Maxwell Award in 2017 for the best book "Human Animal Bond" from the Dog Writers Press. Patti's column "Laws for Paws" appears bi-monthly in the Charleston Gazette-Mail. She also writes a legal column for the Central Pennsylvania Pets Magazine. Visit Patti's site at pattilawson.com.

FOR THE LOVE OF BLIND DOGS:
Dimitri

BY SARAH BARNETT

IT WAS AUGUST OF 2012 when Dimitri was rescued from a puppy mill in Shelby, Ohio, by The Humane Society of the United States in coordination with local organizations. This puppymill had been breeding both shar-peis and chihua-huas, and altogether 200 dogs were ultimately released by the owner.

This particular puppymill owner had previously lived in New Jersey, where she was convicted of animal cruelty and fraud in reference to her dog breeding activities. After ken-nel laws changed in her county, she moved her business to

Richland County, Ohio, where more than 400 dogs ended up living together at one point.

In 2012 her husband died, and she was quite ill herself; when her son came and saw the conditions of the dogs and the property, he reached out for help from the rescue community. As the task was large and overwhelming, The Humane Society of the United States was called in, and many local organizations stepped up to take dogs into their care.

The rescued dogs all presented with a range of health problems; skin problems, heart murmurs, cataracts—quite a few of the dogs were blind because they'd never gotten the much-needed eye surgery to keep their eye lashes from rubbing their eyes, a common problem with shar peis.

Dim, my nickname for Dimitri, suffered from this same physical malady, and when he arrived at the shelter he needed entropian surgery to stop the lashes from digging into his eyes and causing pain. Unfortunately, he already had scarring from many years of this—it was estimated he was between 5 and 7 years old at the time—but the surgery would at least keep it from continuing to happen.

He stayed at the shelter for about a month, as other dogs from the case were adopted out, but he wasn't doing well in the kennels. The shelter reached out to the Lost Dog and Cat Rescue Foundation, which had placed two other shar-peis from the case, to see if they could take him in, since they were a foster-home based rescue. Fortunately for Dim, they said yes.

I had fostered another shar-pei from the case who found a wonderful home. Dim went to his first foster home, but he just didn't adjust well to the other dogs; turned out he wasn't very good at reading social signals.

A month after I took him in to foster, I made the decision to just adopt him myself.

Dim was fearful and easily overstimulated when he first arrived.

When he got excited or very fearful, all sense would just fly out the window, and he'd act out in negative ways. He had poor vision from the scarring in his eyes, which resulted in him running into things, which in turn meant quite a few stitches and staples due to his extremely sensitive skin.

The opthamalogist said his vision would be like seeing through a muddy windshield. The fuzziness of his vision made him more scared about going for walks, loud noises, and new people, than if he couldn't see at all.

Over the next couple years, Dim suffered a few more health issues, such as a tumor that needed to be removed (but was thankfully benign), and shar-pei fever (a condition characterized by recurring fever and swelling of the hocks). He also continued to have eye issues, both pigmentary kera-titis and cataracts. He eventually developed glaucoma and needed surgery to have his eyes removed.

All in all, Dim got the short end of the stick with the genetic lottery, but he just gets through it all, and to this day he remains such an inspiration to me.

Dim was so much happier after his eyes were removed, and he seemed to be more upset by wearing the cone around his neck than by his eyes being gone.

That said, we still had to be really careful with him in new environments. When I took him for walks, I had to make sure to stop him before we went down a set of stairs so that he didn't get completely confused. It took a while, but I was able to teach him the words *Fence* and *Step*.

I tried to balance my close mothering of him in unsafe situations with allowing him his freedom and off-leash time at home on the farm, where he can more confidently prance around the field without hurting himself.

Despite everything he has been through—at the puppy-mill and with all his health issues—Dim still adapts readily to new challenges, and he trusts me, which is an amazing yet scary responsibility. He certainly has his quirks, but honestly, they're what make me love him even more.

Dim does things like carry around his favorite stuffed animal in his mouth all day, or zooms around like a madman when he's very excited.

I remember the first time he grabbed a quesadilla off a plate that was sitting on an ottoman—he was so proud of himself that I couldn't help but laugh. Since then, he's become bolder, and now will put his feet on my lap when I'm eating popcorn and stick his nose in the bowl. He's a surprisingly dainty eater, so I let him do it since he always seems so pleased with himself when he succeeds.

Dim's favorite treat, above all, is soft serve ice cream. I often stop at McDonald's and get him his own cone. He licks it so gently, relishing each bite, taking about ten minutes to finish it while I hold it for him.

The best part about Dim though is his smile. He has this big goofy grin when he's having fun or enjoying himself, and you can't help but smile along with him when you see that precious face.

He's also a great ambassador for puppymill survivors and special needs dogs, in that people can see how quickly they adapt and be less fearful of adopting them. He also raises awareness about what people are really supporting when they purchase a dog online from one of these breeders.

Being able to share Dim's story with people here and on his Facebook page makes me feel like I'm sharing the real and amazingly loving Dim with people. His story has connected me with amazing people with special needs rescue dogs around the world. Sometimes I'll get a message from someone who's read Dim's story on his Facebook page and it helps them feel less fearful as they head into eye removal surgery for their own dog.

I'm so lucky to have him, and hope he inspires other people to adopt, and—especially—to take the leap and adopt blind dogs. As the saying often goes, I'm not sure whether I rescued Dim or he rescued me, but I can tell you he's lit up my life since the day he walked through my front door and straight into my heart.

❦

Sarah Barnett volunteered with the Lost Dog and Cat Rescue Foundation throughout high school and continues to volunteer still today, most recently by helping to manage the farm animal care.

She works at The Humane Society of the United States where Dim accompanies her to work daily, and when she's not at work she is volunteering with causes she believes in, or driving Dim to get ice cream.

MIND OF A MOUSE:
Pez

❦

BY HEATHER LEUGHMYER

FOR AS LONG AS I CAN REMEMBER I have had an affinity for rodents. While others were busy trying to figure out ways to exterminate them, I just wanted to co-exist peacefully. I knew they had a purpose on this earth, and it couldn't be just to annoy or frighten humans.

What must it be like to live your entire life, I wondered, always on high alert, never knowing when a predator was going to appear out of nowhere and make a meal out of you? One second you are simply enjoying the warm sun on your face, and the next, you're in the belly of a killer. Shudder.

Although mice are just as sentient as any other animal, to the rest of the world, their life has little to no value. If they don't end up as food for another, their lives could just as easily end in death by snap trap, glue trap, or poison ingestion.

It always made me sad to see the way these sensitive creatures were being treated, but it never occurred to me that someday my life's mission would include rescuing these incredible little animals.

Pez was surrendered to my rescue, Happy Endings Rat (and also mouse, apparently) Rescue, with his ex-roommate, Dungy. Apparently they had not been able to see eye-to-eye, which is very common with male mice, and they were given their very own bachelor pads. Unfortunately, sweet Dungy had health issues and passed away shortly after arriving at the rescue.

Pez, however, thrived, and it didn't take me long to realize that this handsome little black, white and orange boy (the rat terrier of the mouse world) was no ordinary mouse. Pez was exceptional. In fact, I don't think he even realized he was a mouse—it soon became obvious to me that both Pez and I thought he was just a tiny rat.

In the wild, rats prey on mice, so it is not usually a good idea to let a mouse interact with a full-grown rat; however, there was one rat at my rescue who had been surrendered in deplorable shape and she didn't have an aggressive bone in her emaciated little body. Her name was Noel, and due to her delicate condition I did not think it was a good idea to try and integrate her with my other rats.

I considered her a "hospice" rat, and I knew her time with me was going to be very limited. My goal with her was to make her last days as comfortable and as happy as possible.

She spent a lot of one-on-one time with me, but I thought she might also appreciate meeting a smaller version of herself.

My plan was to introduce Noel to Pez slowly, but Pez had a mind of his own; for him, it was love at first sniff. I let them interact under my supervision several times a day in a neutral setting. Noel tolerated him; she may have even liked him. But it was Pez who was clearly smitten. I would give them each treats like popcorn or potato chips, and while Noel would sit munching away on hers, Pez would take his portion and nudge his way underneath her before eating it. After finishing their treats, Pez would often stay snuggled against her and close his eyes contentedly. Noel pretended not to notice him there, but I couldn't help but think she secretly enjoyed it too.

When Pez wasn't with Noel he was often spending time with me. He loved perching on my shoulder and tunneling through the sleeves of my sweatshirts. Sometimes I would sit at my computer desk and Pez would slide down my leg to the floor and investigate various rooms. He never hid from me as many mice would do. When he was done exploring he would climb back up my leg, get cozy under my hair and take a nap. Being a male, he had a very distinct musky scent that, to me, was strangely pleasant. Even after tucking him in for the night, I could still smell him on my shirt as if he were still there.

One of my favorite games to play with Pez was the tickle game. He would peek out from under my hair and I would gently tickle him as he squeaked happily. He was the only rodent I have ever had who would squeak like this when tickled. It was as if he liked hearing the sound of my laugh as much as I loved hearing his, because he always kept coming back for more. He never seemed to tire of that game and it definitely never got old for me. His antics kept me entertained for hours. How such an enormous personality fit into such a petite little package, I will never comprehend.

I often wondered what was going on in that tiny head of his. How could such a small brain hold so much awareness and intelligence? Pez exhibited more love and emotion in his short time with me than some humans express in their entire lifetime.

Over the years I have had the pleasure of knowing hundreds of beautiful rescue rodents, but Pez will always remain one of the most memorable. My experience with him is something I know can never be duplicated. That delightful and endearing little guy took a piece of my heart with him when he left this world, and I know without a doubt, there will never be another quite like Pez.

☙❧

Heather Leughmyer is the author of *Adopting Adele, Brave Benny, A Rat's Guide to Owning a Human,* and *If Your Tears Were Human,* and co-editor of *Rescue Smiles.* She is also the founder of Happy Endings Rat Rescue, and a graduate of Indiana-Purdue University with a B.A. in Writing and Linguistics.

Writing has been a passion of hers for as long as she has advocated for animals.

She lives in Columbia City, Indiana, with her husband, daughter, and several animal companions.

Everlasting Love:
Hope

by Joe Maringo

Most of my rescues and associated stories start out in some way with social media, and this one is no exception. While cruising Facebook one morning I came across a picture of a sad-looking, fuzzy black lab mix. I see dozens of these dogs every time I log onto the computer, so I don't know why this one stood out to me, but it did.

It was a posting by a girl named Nicole in Ohio who was asking for someone to help the beautiful old soul that was pictured. Reading her story I found that the dog's name was Hope, and she was listed at the Stark County Dog Pound in

Ohio. Hope had been there for a while, and there was slim chance of her ever finding a home. She had very little fur due to flea infestation and was thin and a bit arthritic—oh, and by the way, Hope was nineteen years old!

I paused at this point, "Nineteen?!" How could anyone leave a dog that age just sit in the pound and wait for the end to come? I made the decision right then and there that Hope would be with us as soon as the shelter opened the next day.

I started to message back and forth with Nicole and found that Hope had some health issues that needed to be addressed. Nicole was a volunteer at the shelter, but was also in the vet tech program at a local school. Hope was brought to the school to have her health accessed and any possible treatments done. Her biggest hurdle was that she was heart-worm positive.

This was a heartbreaking bit of information as the typical treatment for heartworm is a series of very painful injec-tions in the muscles that run along the spine. There is no way a dog in Hope's condition and of her age could survive the usual treatment. She also had severe flea dermatitis, was underweight, and had a very large tumor on her front leg. Making it even sadder, Nicole assured me that Hope was just as sweet as could be and loved everyone.

I sat back and read through the 100-plus replies of people who had pledged to donate to anyone who could save Hope, and calls for someone to just give her a place to lay her head for her final days. Sadly, there were no offers to just bring her home and love her for the rest of her time—that is, until I posted my comment.

We started the Shades Of Grey Sanctuary for senior dogs in 2009 to help weary and broken dogs in exactly these types of situations. We almost always have between twelve and fifteen seniors living peacefully in my home, and bringing one more in would not unduly add to the stress or workload. It would be my honor to give Hope the life she deserved for whatever time she had left.

I made plans with Nicole, and though I found out the shelter was closed the next day, I would be there when the doors opened on Monday. There were a few challenges though. I was told through various sources that the shelter was not particularly rescue-friendly. Hope would be available to the first person in line that wanted her with no questions asked. If by chance someone got there ahead of me who wanted her, I would be out of luck.

I also discovered that they would not hold Hope if I called them, so I had to make the three hour drive under the assumption that she would still be there when I got there. I nervously waited for the time to come and then messaged all my new friends and supporters that I was on my way; the next time they would hear from me would be with a picture of Hope in my truck. I decided to video the entire rescue so everyone could experience the joy of her freedom ride just as I would.

I arrived at the shelter an hour before it opened to the public. I noticed people going in and out so figured I would give it a try. The doors were open and they had volunteers cleaning and caring for the animals in the shelter. I asked who was in charge, and told them who I was. Their reply right away was, "Oh, you are the guy who wants Hope." I guess the news had spread far and wide and had made it to the shelter long before I did.

They informed me that several people had called about

her. My heart sank, fearing that they would give her to someone else, or may have already done so.

"I am first in line for her though, right?" My nerves were showing. Once I'd made the commitment to rescuing Hope, in my mind she was already mine, so the thought of her going with someone else was painful. Not only that, but I wanted to spoil her and give her the life of her doggie dreams.

"Yes, you're the first one here, so she's all yours if you still want her after you see her. But we're not officially open for another hour, so you'll have to come back then." I went back out to the truck, made some video, and nervously waited. The minutes crawled by, but the time finally came for the shelter to be open to the public.

I went back in and asked to meet Hope. My heart sank yet again, as now they told me Hope was not back from the vet school yet. They were running late and were supposed to have been back awhile ago. I would just have to sit some more, but they said I could do the paperwork while I waited.

While I was on hold, I watched as people came and went. A few dogs got adopted, and some people left empty-handed. I watched a younger girl come in and walk to the desk, and then I heard her say "I'm here to adopt Hope."

My heart dropped, and I became extremely nervous, as there was still a chance I might miss out. What if this girl was connected to someone there and was bumped ahead of me? In rescue you learn nothing is ever a sure thing until the dog is in your truck and you are headed home. I was relieved to hear them tell her she was second in line. I waited and it seemed to take forever, but then I heard them say the van had pulled in.

A man walked through the front door, and they looked at me and said "There's your girl."

I was somewhat shocked. She was so small, much smaller than I had thought. She weighed just 23 pounds. She had very little hair, and when I went to hug her she let out a loud yelp. She had horrible ear infections. All in all though, she was beautiful. She enjoyed the soft petting and we finished the paperwork and did the obligatory exit photo. Looking at her paperwork it actually had a birthdate listed of February 6, 1995. WOW! She really was nineteen years old.

I also found she had been at the shelter for almost a month, and was a cruelty confiscation. The poor old soul had been sitting there alone and lonely for a month before Nicole stepped forward to try to find help for her. I give Nicole the credit for saving Hope, I was just the one who gave her a place to go.

I hooked her leash onto her pretty new rainbow colored collar, on the ring that carried a nametag that simply said HOPE. We walked out the door, and SHE pulled ME to the truck. My truck sits very high—much too high for her to jump in—but when I opened the door she gave it a try anyway. I caught her midair and lifted her up and in. She met my Sammy who was in the front seat, made one or two circles and settled in for the ride home. I had been videoing all the phases of her freedom, so I quickly put it together and hit send so all our supporters and Hope's new friends could witness her happiness.

When we arrived at my house I introduced her to the rest of the seniors. She walked in, said to everyone "I AM HOME" and has never looked back. She had a nice stroll around the yard, found a soft clump of grass, and flopped over for a long roll. That was the moment I learned that this is her favorite thing to do. She drops over at any moment and rolls while making a whining sound of pure joy.

It doesn't matter whether it's grass, dirt, mud, or snow, it's all the same to her and she rolls wherever she is. Sometimes she will even start at the top of a hill and roll all the way to the bottom, which never fails to bring a wide grin to both of our faces.

Our first order of business once she got situated was to get her to our vet. We knew she could not survive the standard heartworm treatment, so I discussed using what has become known in the rescue community as the "slow kill method" for her. It would be easier on her system and she could continue to enjoy her new life rather than being caged up for six or eight more weeks, if there was even a chance of her surviving it. At this point we did not know if Hope had days, weeks or more with us. After all, she was already nineteen; how much longer could she go on?

We addressed her sore and infected ears, put her on a course of antibiotics for her skin issues, and then had a look at the tumor on her leg. That was the issue of immediate concern, and we quickly determined that it was a slow growing but malignant Spindle Cell Carcinoma. Yep, the "C" word, cancer. This was made even worse because her heartworm would compromise her blood flow and ability to get oxygen into her blood, so anesthesia was out of the question. We couldn't feasibly remove her tumor, at least not at that time.

It was not all the best of news, but all things considered, it could have been worse.

Next we went for a nice grooming at The Barker Shop

with some medicated shampoo to try to help with the itching and hair loss. It was obvious that she'd had a flea problem, and probably for quite some time. Hope particularly enjoyed the spa treatment, just like the pampered princess she deserved to be. The girls at the groomer are always kind and gentle to all the dogs that go there, but they really gave Hope the royal treatment. She looked like a different dog after her grooming. She had even less hair, but she had a smile and an attitude that said, "I am the queen, just look at me!"

She certainly was the queen, and that quickly became one of my favorite nicknames for her.

She settled into a routine with us and enjoyed each day as it came. We always wondered how long she would hang on, but it seemed like she was just improving and getting stronger with time. She was even feeling well enough to start going for regular rides in the truck with Sammy and I.

Sammy was my right-arm man. He is my constant companion and he goes everywhere that I go. Hope loved the rides, and loved meeting new people, who were always amazed at her age and vigor. She also came to love Wednesdays, because Wednesday was my day to have sushi for lunch, and I always made sure to order a California roll for each dog. Sammy knew the routine and always waited for his, but Hope's first few times she just looked at me as if to ask, "Is this really all for me?" Then she would happily devour her treat.

Months went by and Hope continued to thrive. She gained weight, her hair thickened a little bit and her ears cleared up. Her tumor remained the same size but her heartworm continued to be an issue. We have used the slow kill method on dozens of dogs, and all have been negative after six months of treatment, but not Miss Hope. She still tested a strong positive, so we continued the slow treatment praying that we'd have better luck in the next six months.

Summer passed and turned to fall, and Hope started to shed her sparse hair. I worried she might be naked for winter, but her coat came back in a little thicker than it had been. I was happy she would have some protection from the cold Pennsylvania winter, but I also bought her a fleece coat to wear on those extra cold days. It also became common practice for her to sleep curled up next to my head in bed, sharing my pillow. I could keep track of her easily that way, and if she started to shiver I could share my blanket with her.

The first anniversary of her rescue was quite a big deal for us. It was just a few weeks from her actual birthday, so we combined the celebrations. We threw her a party, shared her video to all her friends and supporters, and we commented on how amazing it was that Hope was now twenty years old. She had settled in as our official greeter and our senior ambassador along with Sammy when we did events.

Hope loved meeting new people, especially kids. She was determined that she was going to make up for all the petting she had missed out on in her first nineteen years.

Hope again shed her winter coat that spring, and what came back in was a surprise to everyone. Her previous coats had always been thin, and quickly became oily and matted easily. This shedding was different though. Hope's new coat was like a newly planted lawn, with the first little green sprouts poking their noses out into the world. It was coming in full and thick and in places there had never been hair since the day I'd met her! Over the course of several weeks it came in so thick that people didn't recognize her, and thought she was a different dog. She was now as beautiful physically as she was on the inside. We started to brush her long fur regularly, and she preened under the pampering.

It took almost eighteen months for her heartworm test to come back negative. That was yet another cause for celebration, but it was tempered by the fact that the tumor on her leg had started to grow, and was now too intertwined with the muscle to ever be removed. I don't believe I would have felt comfortable putting a twenty-year-old dog under for the surgery, anyway, so we let it be what it would be and were grateful for all the months she'd had with us.

Hope is still with us at Shades of Grey as I write. She has had many adventures, has traveled all over the east coast, met hundreds of new people, gone swimming in Lake Erie, and ruled our home and the other dogs there like the Grand Lady that she is.

She is mostly deaf now, but she does have those days where she can hear a bit if I yell loud enough. She has become night blind and I have to be careful letting her out after dark so she does not run into things. She is still my Queen and still loves to roll. Her Twenty Second, YES, TWENTY-SECOND birthday, is just weeks away. It's a milestone that no dog I have ever known has come close to, and it's a testament to this little girl's spirit and tenacity.

Wouldn't it be great if all dogs could be with us as long as Hope Everlasting!

ꙮ

Joe Maringo is the Director of Southwest Pennsylvania Retriever Rescue Org/S.P.A.R.R.O. and Shades of Grey Sanctuary For Senior Dogs in Plum, Pennsylvania. Over the years SPARRO has grown and to date they have rescued over 1,000 dogs, from every single state east of the Rockies and from Canada as well. Donate for their rescue efforts at www.sparro.org.

INSEPARABLE SURPRISES:
Cissy and Missy

BY BARB MICHAEL

CISSY AND MISSY WERE ADOPTED at six months of age from a very kind, older couple, the Martins. Mr. and Mrs. Martin were quite generous people, and they opened their home to many animals in need. They told us they had soft spots in their hearts for animals, and that they did! They had several dogs and cats of their own they had adopted, too.

They lived beside a river and made daily trips to a local discount bread store, purchasing trays of leftover bread for their duck friends. The ducks knew the schedule and arrived on time each evening for their treats. We got to witness this heartwarming event one night after meeting the couple, and we stood and watched with them as the many ducks swam or flew in to gobble up the bread tossed their way.

The Martins also had a barn at the back of their property where feral cats could freely roam in and out at will. They trapped them when they were able and had them spayed and/or neutered to keep the population in check.

They purchase cat food and litter out of their own pockets, too, and one of their many tasks was to feed, water, and change several litter trays in the barn for these cats each day.

One evening, Mr. Martin noticed the feral cat they took to calling Sweet Mama (they all had names) was nursing a new baby kitten. He observed her nursing the same, single kitten the following day. When he arrived in the barn on the second day after the kitten's appearance, Sweet Mama was now nursing two kittens. From that, Mr. Martin believed the kittens were born two days apart.

Mr. and Mrs. Martin continued to monitor these new kittens and began giving them human contact when their mama would leave them in their little corner for a short while. They would talk to them, pet them, and begin to get them used to hearing human voices and accepting human touch. They continued this practice until they were weaned and able to eat on their own.

At that time, the Martins moved the two little girls into the home with them, caring for them and getting them used to living inside until they felt they were ready for a forever home.

At that time, they placed an advertisement in the local newspaper, and we answered it.

As soon as we went to meet the little darlings, we couldn't resist taking them home with us. Since they were bonded and had always been together, it was the Martins' wish that they stay together, and it was our wish as well.

The Martins had repeated this process many times with other feral cats, finding adoptive homes for their kittens and getting the parents spayed and neutered. They also would pay for shots and sterilization of the kittens, too. Although they strongly objected, we insisted that we would pay the expenses of these two kittens, and that they could use it for other kitties in need. They reluctantly agreed.

Although Cissy and Missy are now grown, they still eat together, play together, sleep together and love each other dearly. Cissy is the shyer of the two and always needs Missy by her side; however, neither of them is fond of strangers and will hide together when company comes over.

The girls are as happy with us as we are with them, and they definitely know how to purr! They are similar enough in looks, with their white fur and black markings, that they make for gorgeous pictures as they lay together in the sink, or hang out on the cat tree together.

The Martins came to visit Cissy and Missy once after we adopted them. The couple's eyes lit up when they saw the girls, and as they were petting them and fussing over them, they told us how pleased they were that we had given them such a loving home. It meant a lot to them.

The Martins not only went above and beyond for animals, but they also helped people. At one point they opened their home to a Cambodian family of eight that had escaped the war and was being sponsored by their church. The family lived with the Martins for six months until the father found employment and they were able to find other housing.

Mrs. Martin passed away a few years ago with an inoperable brain tumor and Mr. Martin now resides in a nursing home in poor health. They will both be remembered for the good things they did for our planet's residents, human and animals alike. We thank Mr. and Mrs. Martin, Cissy and Missy thank them, and many, many more animals and people thank them for their wonderful, unselfish kindness!

This world would benefit greatly with more loving, caring, generous folks like them.

⊗⊗

Barbara Michael lives in Warsaw, Indiana with her husband of 51 years, a collie dog named Lacie, and Cissy and Missy, her two adopted kitties. She has two married daughters and three grandchildren. She is retired from a local bank and makes hand-embellished hair accessories and hats, greeting cards, and sells them along with other unique baby items in craft stores.

CATALYSTS FOR CHANGE:
Cinnamon and Spice

BY SUNNY ARIS

IT WAS AUGUST OF 2010, and two sisters were about to be executed by conservation officers on the Mescalero Reservation in New Mexico.

Who ordered the shooting death of these 6-year-old dogs? Why, the very same woman whose dog gave birth to them—and dozens of other puppies. At this point, any sane and reasonable person might ask why she would do such a thing. The answer to that was simple: because both dogs were about to deliver more puppies, of course.

That's how it works on the reservation. If you want your old, injured, or unwanted animals killed, you simply call the officers and get your name added to the list.

This woman wanted to make sure that this would happen before the girls had their puppies, so she lied, claiming they were "vicious." She knew that a vicious dog gets you to the top of the list so that you don't have to wait for months. I was surprised she didn't just release them as stray, given that the officers regularly drove around at night, shot every stray dog and cat they saw, and then piled their dead bodies next to the dumpsters.

Making matters worse, the children of the reservation had to walk by these dumpsters—and therefore the dead animals—on their way to school. Can you imagine a little child forced to witness his or her beloved kitten or puppy lying dead by the dumpster, and then have to continue on to school as though all was well? It was beyond inhumane to the animals, and abusive to the children, too.

We begged the president of the tribe to end this practice. There was even a newspaper article about it in the Ruidoso News asking for the chilling cruelty to stop. But instead of ending the culls, a new dump was created behind the existing dump with a lime pit to dispose of the bodies, so that the children wouldn't see them anymore.

At that time, I was producing an animal welfare radio show in Southeastern New Mexico, and my home was just minutes from the reservation. A caller informed me of the girls' plight. He told me that they were not vicious, and in fact, came to his home every day to get food from his porch and play with his dog. "They're terrified of people, and with good reason, but they are not mean at all," he said, begging me to help them.

My friend and partner in crime, Nancy Berg, fellow cofounder of the local spay-neuter program, was aghast. We decided that something needed to be done, and so drove to the reservation to meet the dogs. When we saw the girls we immediately fell in love. They both shook and snarled, but took the food we laid down.

The bigger and bossier of the two, who we would later name "Cinnamon", took food from my hand. I melted. Spice (the thinner and more malnourished of the two), desperately wanted the food but was too frightened to do anything but shiver and drool in the background.

We begged for a stay of execution from the conservation officers and got "three days max." We immediately went to work on a rescue that would change many lives—including our own—for years to come; we just didn't know it yet. Three days later, friends had built birthing areas in a side yard at my Ruidoso home, and we were spending hours each day trying to get close enough to catch the starving sisters.

☾☯︎

On the third day, one hour before they were to be shot, we finally lured the girls into our old food transport van. We'd done it! I can still remember the feeling of joy as we celebrated our victory. We'd saved their lives. The high was indescribable.

Now that we had them in our protective custody, we promptly headed off to the only veterinarian who would see them: a country vet an hour away. "You'll be lucky if you have 36 hours before they deliver," Dr. Washburn said sadly, "and if that one survives the births, it will be a miracle."

She was pointing to Spice, who looked like a pregnant skeleton with huge eyes. She gave them parvo-distemper shots, and then we headed back toward my home to make them comfortable in the birthing sheds that had been built just for them, her last words ringing in our ears. "Hopefully if the skinny one dies, the other one can care for her pups."

It wasn't what we wanted to hear, but exactly what we had feared, so we emotionally prepared ourselves for the worst and hoped for the best.

Back in Ruidoso, Nancy was waiting to greet our new residents with a huge pot of chicken soup. I'm here to tell you, never had a pot of soup disappeared faster! It did our hearts good to see them eating, and eating heartily.

We got lucky. Despite the vet's opinion, and the fact that we could easily see the babies moving, the girls held on to those babies for another two weeks. That gave them the time they needed to put on some desperately needed weight and grow stronger. In the meantime, even Spice was slowly getting over her fear and warming up to us. We were hopeful.

In the early morning hours of August 24th, Cinnamon delivered nine puppies. She stood up while she delivered each one, which is typical of feral dog behavior. On August 27th, Spice followed suit, outdoing her sister by popping out eleven puppies. Three were stillborn, leaving us with seventeen babies altogether— all immune compromised—but all of whom we were bound and determined to keep alive.

The next weeks proved to be a whirlwind of hard work and excitement: watching the babies grow, thrive, and play, and giggling like schoolgirls as Cinnamon stole Spice's babies one at a time as if they were hers all along.

The puppies all survived, miraculously, and were adopted into loving homes. Now, it was time to have the sisters spayed and put an end to this cruel breeding cycle. Their health was still poor, however, due to nursing the puppies and getting them through their first eight weeks. So we set out to bring both moms back to good health before putting them on the operating table. Our recipe was this: pots and pots of home-made chicken and rice soup, high-quality kibble, and Super Blue Green algae with probiotics.

Their care also included prayers by those who felt led to do so, and lots of TLC. They had visitors daily in order to get them socialized, and they were gradually coming around more and more toward the behavior of "normal" dogs.

After seeing the sisters' uteruses, the veterinarian esti-mated that each had given birth to at least ten litters! We were floored. Dr. Washburn told us that Spice's uterus was so fragile it was like "tissue paper." In addition, the vet took dozens of BB pellets out of both dogs, but many were too close to major organs to remove safely and had to be left in place.

After months of daily care and worry for just these two dogs—and the stress of dealing with the behavioral quirks caused by years of abuse—Nancy and I knew that this cruel-ty and death could not continue unchecked. Something had to be done. Not just about the reservation, but the 135,000 pets being abandoned in New Mexico every single year.

We thought long and hard about it, but ultimately agreed that we were ready: Cinnamon and Spice became the inspi-ration for Animal Village NM, and both girls' paw prints are forever captured in cement where their birthing areas used to be.

We soon purchased a 9-acre property on a busy New Mexico highway and within a week, we had more than 100 dogs and cats. "Cinny" and Spice helped us to realize the scope of the problem; that abandonment, cruelty, ignorance, lack of education, poverty, and lack of appropriate laws all work together to create a nightmare for helpless animals.

Ironically enough, the same woman who had ordered them killed came to us one day looking to adopt. "That one wouldn't go away from her mommy (me)," the woman said, pointing to Spice. "My husband was drunk one night and hit her on the head with a shovel. He said maybe now she'll stay away. He was right. She did." That explained why Spice's head was slightly tilted.

At that point, the woman was escorted from our property with explicit instructions never to return.

Spice and Cinnamon were front and center the November night we opened the Village in 2010, and although we were overjoyed when they both got adopted that evening, we were yet still so naïve in believing that most people would love and care for their dogs as we would. That would be another lesson.

Today, Spice is back with us, after she was found running the streets of Ruidoso, abandoned once again. We re-rescued our precious Spice, now ten years old, and once again she was left sickly and emaciated, this time by someone we'd trusted to care for her. I was heartbroken!

Luckily, she recognized me immediately, gobbled down the food I'd brought with me, and over the next few weeks, she came back to health and even got the sparkle back in her eye.

Spice is a living metaphor for our no-kill shelter. Time and again, our shelter has gone through trials that would have put most people out of business. Our shelter continues to starve for funding in America's poorest state, as the abuse and overbreeding that almost killed these incredibly loyal sisters is still rampant.

But when I look at Spice's face and watch her silly antics here at Animal Village NM—where she is much loved by staff—I know that it has all been worth it. I don't know if Spice will ever be adopted again at her age; not all of them will find forever homes.

I believe that these dogs and cats were put here to show humans what unconditional love really looks like, and I hope that we rescuers will be welcomed in Heaven by the wonderful animals we believe in on earth.

These two sisters deserved another chance, and became my inspiration to do more for others like them. Don't they all deserve the best life has to offer?

🐾

Sunny Aris is the co-founder and Director of Animal Village NM. Animal Village NM is a 501(c)(3) non-profit, no-kill shelter located at 7246 Highway 54-70, Alamogordo, NM 88310. To learn more or donate for their work, visit www.AnimalVillageNM.org.

HER GIFT TO ME:
Miss Rat

BY CHRISTOPHER C. BARNEKOV

I BURIED MY PRECIOUS LITTLE SWEETHEART last week. Miss Rat lost her brave, ten-month battle against a succession of tumors, and I knew we'd both given it our all. At 35 months, she'd survived her third surgery, but her tired little body just couldn't repair the damage the tumor had done. She was a sweetheart to the end, snuggling and bruxing for me even the morning she passed.

I never intended to become a rat aficionado. In the previous 56 years I'd lived on the planet, I'd never had a pet, and was not interested in having one. Miss Rat came into my home by surprise, perched on the arm of Kevin, the youngest of three boys I'd raised, all "rescues" from fatherless homes themselves.

Yet here I was, immediately taken with Miss Rat. I had never seen such a cute little creature, and I could sense she had a truly unique and sweet spirit.

Not knowing any better at the time, at first Miss Rat was confined alone in a small aquarium most of the day, and fed gerbil food. Our relationship truly began the day I offered her a little piece of fresh broccoli. She was thrilled, and it touched my heart!

I began visiting with her as I could when Kevin was busy. It didn't take long for her to conquer my heart—after just a few weeks, I couldn't stand leaving her in that tiny aquarium any longer, so I bought the roomiest cage I could find.

I even started cleaning her cage so she'd have fresh bedding—all the while still telling myself she was Kevin's companion, not mine.

Many months later, Kevin decided he wanted to move into the college dorms. Miss Rat needed a "rescue," and since I was already attached to her despite my best intentions, I adopted her at once and began studying rat care in earnest.

To my chagrin, the first thing I learned was that rats are highly intelligent, highly social creatures that should *never* be kept alone. But Miss Rat was now full grown, which presented a dilemma. I read about the risks of introducing new rats, and didn't want any harm to come to her.

What to do? I couldn't stand the thought that she was lonely and bored, but I was afraid to risk introducing a companion.

I decided to become her companion myself and see if

that would work. I'm a sorry excuse for a real rat, but she never complained. I made a point of spending as much time as possible with her, converting our TV room into a safe rat playground so we could be together. I let her run free in there four or five hours a night, watching her antics and interacting with her, at the expense of several projects I'd previously taken on.

Miss Rat thoughtfully confined her destructive efforts to one old sofa, in which she built a nest that was an awesome achievement of rat architecture. I finally dismantled it (and the sofa) after her second tumor surgery, when she retired permanently to warmer and safer quarters in my bedroom/office.

Miss Rat was always sweet, never complaining, even when left alone for many hours. Of course, she was a true rat, and so perpetrated the obligatory mischief as the occasion warranted. But it was an old sofa, and the custom hole in the shoulder of that new shirt made it my favorite. The pants she perforated were much cooler afterwards. She was a great help to me in keeping clutter off my desk, and I always knew I could find that missing item in her treasure stash. All these services were provided with such sweetness and innocence that they were a real delight. She had built a grand nest in my heart.

After her second surgery, Miss Rat lost much of her stamina. She could no longer climb, so I built a large, six-level complex of ramps around my desk. To make her life easier, there were "rest rooms" and water stations on three levels. As she weakened, I made the ramps longer and less steep and added non-slip strips. Because she could not climb down to the floor, she had free range of her extensive domain, and enjoyed it greatly.

As her health continued to fail both of us, we bonded even more tightly. With her nests surrounding my desk, we spent even more time together, especially since I was able to telecommute two days a week. Miss Rat could even get to my bed, and most nights she visited once or twice for snuggles, snacks, and scritches (my impeccably mannered little sweetheart returned to her "rest room" as necessary, and had only one very slight accident in six months). I gladly lost a lot of sleep, and gained a lot of love.

Of course, I saw that she could not last much longer. We tried every therapy, but the tumors returned. At her age, her vet and I were afraid to risk another surgery. We were enjoying each other, and as long as she was not in pain, I feared risking losing her prematurely.

Until just recently, Miss Rat enjoyed our life and simple bond of love. As Miss Rat grew weaker, my love grew stronger, and I delighted in caring for her. I prepared gourmet rat feasts, and she gave high praise to my catering services. I found many ways to pamper and comfort her, and these gifts were a source of comfort to my soul.

I realized that I was setting myself up for a devastating emotional blow when the inevitable time of her death arrived. I spared no effort or expense to put off that day, but knew it was coming regardless. This was intensely painful for me.

Often I became so distraught I could barely breathe. Many nights I sobbed uncontrollably, thinking of my life without her in it. As I write, it has been a week since she left me, and I still break down often thinking of her. Writing about her has cost me a box of Kleenex.

I suppose I've lived a sheltered life, but I have never felt such intense pain. This, I've now realized, is why I was always afraid to have a pet. I didn't think I could bear the loss.

Yet, I've also learned that I would not have missed this experience for anything, and I'm so grateful for it. Miss Rat gave me many precious gifts, the most precious of which is spiritual: Miss Rat helped me understand God's love.

Miss Rat was 'only' a rodent. Her skills were pretty much limited to slinking, snatching, and shredding. Her life span was at most 30 to 40 months. Yet I loved this little rodent so intensely, so profoundly, that I gladly sacrificed vast quantities of time, effort, attention, and money to try to cure her and care for her. I joyously spared no expense. I would gladly have sacrificed much, much more if there was any chance at all it would help even a little. I loved Miss Rat with all my heart, and soul and mind.

Gradually, I came to realize what God was showing me through Miss Rat. As powerful as my feelings for Miss Rat were, they paled in comparison to God's love. This knowledge in and of itself served as a great comfort to me.

I buried Miss Rat's little body. She was laid to rest in a very special spot in my shade garden, in a little casket (a true treasure box). I suspect that no rat has ever been given such a burial, nor mourned more profoundly, yet this seemed only fitting.

When I arrive in heaven, I will be overjoyed, but not surprised, if Miss Rat is waiting to welcome and guide me "further up and further in."

I can't be sure that this is God's plan, but all I have learned about Him in 36 years as a believer persuades me that, if not, it is only because He is planning something even better than I can imagine right now.

૭૯

Dr. Barnekov earned his PhD in Economics at the University of Chicago. He has taught economics at Ohio State University and Ohio University, served six years as editor of Evangel, the magazine of The American Association of Lutheran Churches, and is now retired after serving as a senior economist at the Federal Communications Commission.

DYING TO LIVE:
Gene-o

BY GAYLA FRANCES EVANS

I'LL NEVER FORGET THAT DAY. It was April 17th, the anniversary of my father Eugene's death, and somehow it went from ordinary to extraordinary. I usually don't do much that day; maybe look at family pictures and reminisce about my father's life, or even visit him at the grave site. For the most part, I am content to just be alone on this sad day.

For some reason, on this particular anniversary, I decided to do something I normally wouldn't do and surf the internet. Upon logging onto the computer, the first thing I saw was a photo of Gene-o.

As I stared at his abused, emaciated body I was overwhelmed with emotions. The tears began to flow and I was at a complete loss for words. This was a dog who suffered 24 hours a day at the end of a chain, weak and slowly dying, with an embedded collar around his neck. His "owner" even went as far as shooting him in the neck in an attempt to kill him. Gene-o had no food, water, or shelter and was fighting the elements daily just to survive.

I was grateful for the neighbor who tried to help him by setting up a make-shift shelter to keep him as dry as possible as he lay listlessly on the muddy ground, his head in the rain, water dripping from a despondent face. He looked as though he was ready to just give up.

When his rescuer got closer to him she could smell the stench of death. His neck was wrapped in an ace bandage and as he let her remove it, the source of the smell became obvious. She called the authorities, who came and removed him immediately. That's when they contacted me.

They began treating his neck for infection and kept him as comfortable as possible until I could make arrangements to make the drive to get him. Gene-o was grossly underweight at only 60 pounds, anemic, infested with fleas, full of worms and heartworm positive. He was missing fur, both his ears and his neck were infected, and he had been shot in the neck with a .32 caliber.

Gene-o had to put on weight before he could even be treated for heartworm. His treatment was intense and very hard on his already-abused body, but he eventually pulled out of it. After that, the bullet was removed and he was neutered, given his shots, and microchipped.

It took a full year for Gene-o to finally come back to health. He went from 60 to 105 pounds, and became a very happy and (rightfully) spoiled boy. I watched as he learned how to be a real dog and how to play. He had never experienced human kindness, or been given a toy to play with. The first time he saw a ball he wasn't even sure what to do with it—but it wasn't long before a ball became one of his favorite toys.

Many years ago when I was very young we lived next door to an Italian family who kept an abundant garden. The woman would often bring baskets full of vegetables to us, and when she saw my dad in the yard she would shout, "Hey Gene-o! I have some vegetables for you!" I thought this name was fitting for the dog who came to me on the day my father left this world.

Now, when April 17th rolls around, I smile. It is no longer a day full of sadness, it is a day full of hope; a day that made a huge difference in the life of one very special dog and a day that also made a big difference for my grieving heart. Although Gene-o had a difficult start in life, time healed his wounds, both physically and mentally. Even after being so neglected and abused, he still has so much love to give.

Thank you, Dad, for looking down on me and Gene-o—a dog dying to live.

⊗

Gayla Frances Evans is Founder and President of Ohio Rottweiler Rescue. You can contact her at Rottrod2@aol.com for more info or to donate for their work.

UNCOMPROMISED COMPASSION:
Layla, Ricky, and Lucy

BY ANDEE BINGHAM

LAYLA, RICKY, AND LUCY **FOUND THEIR WAY** to Brother Wolf's Animal Sanctuary when a family saw them being sold on the side of the road as "feed pigs". Their empathetic child saw what fate the piglets faced and begged for their lives. The family turned their car around, made a deal with the farmer, and then delivered them to us.

Laura, Brother Wolf's education outreach manager, spends a lot of her time caring for and building relationships with the animals at the Sanctuary. "When Layla, Ricky, and Lucy came to us they were very small and affectionate," she says. "Almost anybody could go into their pen to play with them. They got big quickly, but their behaviors were still the same. At feeding time, we'd walk into the pen and they'd be so excited because pigs are very food motivated. In their eagerness, it was easy to get knocked over since they're so big."

As work on the Brother Wolf Sanctuary amps up, there will be more and more visitors who will want to interact with the animals. Laura knew something needed to change if those interactions were going to be safe for everyone. "I thought maybe I could teach them to sit for their food," she says, "and I was delighted to see how quickly Layla caught on!"

First, Laura went into the pen with a container of diced up apples. "Of course they got really excited because they knew I had treats. I stood in front of them like I would with a dog, using a commanding posture. Then I held the treat in my closed hand and moved forward until Layla's head tilted up. I kept moving my fist forward until she backed up into the seated position. Once she was there, she got the treat."

Even though Layla caught on quick, Laura admits it's a work in progress for Ricky and Lucy. "It's hard because they're very excitable. Ricky and Lucy are going to take more time. Ricky is almost getting it, he's almost there. He'll back up and his legs will start to go down, but then he'll get distracted. We're working on it."

Layla hasn't exactly been tolerant of the slower progress of her friends. "Now that Layla knows how to sit she can be impatient. For example, now when I'm working with the other pigs to teach them, Layla is already sitting behind me being like—'Hey, I'm ready. I'm doing what I'm supposed to be doing. Where's my treat?'"

While the end goal of this exercise is to teach them to sit for their food, Laura is quick to point out that "the objective isn't to get them to do tricks. The intention is to provide mental stimulation and to create a pattern that will allow other people to interact with them safely."

"When they hear the clang of the fence opening, they come running to me," Laura says. "It's just like when you come home from a day of work and your dog greets you at the door. They're just so happy. People have dogs at home who do the exact same thing, so I'm hoping people will make that connection."

That's not the only way pigs are a lot like dogs. "If you rub on their bellies or sides enough, they'll lay down and fall asleep, just like a dog. Layla, Ricky, and Lucy will all do it. They're going to fall asleep if they're being loved on by someone that they know and trust. They also love being scratched behind their ears."

"I just want people to realize that these are sentient beings who want to live too," Laura says. "I want people to see how similar they are to companion animals. Nobody would want to see their dog being abused or sold on the side of the road as food. Layla, Ricky, and Lucy deserve the same respect we give the dogs and cats in our care."

Layla, Ricky, and Lucy will be just a few of the precious souls visitors to the Sanctuary will get to meet starting in 2018. The Sanctuary will be an educational hub that'll provide a spacious, serene environment for animals of all walks of life.

"People smile right away when they see the pigs," Laura says. "They see how excited they are, and that happiness is contagious. If everyone can experience that and think about how special they are, that will be awesome."

❦

Andee Bingham is the staff writer for Brother Wolf Animal Rescue. BWAR was founded in 2007 to provide the programs and resources necessary to build No-Kill communities. The organization is currently building an 82.5-acre Sanctuary for our dogs and cats, as well as a variety of farmed animals. The Sanctuary will provide critical care for animals who have been so abused and neglected that they require longer term, more specialized rehabilitation. In addition, the Sanctuary's Learning Center will be an educational resource for visitors to learn about our responsibilities to animals, our environment, and society. Visit www.bwar.org/sanctuary to learn more.

A Feral Princess:
Bootsie, aka Tootance

by Tamira Thayne

Most animal rescuers in America are familiar with or have dealt with their fair share of feral cat conundrums. For anyone who might not know what feral means with regards to cats, ferals are those who are born outdoors and as a result get no interaction or socialization with people—they are essentially wild animals.

It becomes much more difficult to tame a feral cat once they've gone beyond the kitten stage, when they will readily adjust to living with and enjoying the company of humans.

When I moved my chained-dog rescue organization from Pennsylvania to Virginia, I stopped doing any cat rescue. We had a house full of formerly neglected dogs, and the three cats that made the move with us stayed with me upstairs in the master bedroom where it was safer for them.

However, back in Pennsylvania, the organization's treasurer ended up with a budding cat colony in her backyard. She had a feral momma cat move in nearby that she was trying to catch and spay. But the momma was smart and avoided the trap, birthing two litters back to back that Deb then had to catch and spay, too. It seemed a never-ending battle.

By the time Deb trapped Bootsie she was already seven months old—well beyond the age at which most ferals are able to be tamed.

Compounding the problem, the vet believed her to be pregnant, and so decisions had to be made quickly as far as how to proceed. Obviously she couldn't be released back into the wild in her pregnant state, but neither Deb nor I felt comfortable with the other option either. I decided to bring her to the center and keep her in one of the large upstairs bathrooms until she gave birth, then adopt out the kittens and get her spayed.

I hoped to tame her while she was my captive audience, too.

I began by just hanging out in the same room with her in the evenings. It was peaceful up there in that bathroom, just she and I, quietly co-existing. Before long, though, she was climbing into my lap and rubbing her face up against mine, even letting me pet her a little. I was shocked and elated!

A month went by, and I didn't feel any movement that

signaled kittens inside her; she didn't seem to be expanding, her nipples weren't engorged. I consulted "the Google" and found that the gestation period for a cat is 63-65 days. She should have been ready to pop by this time—yet I was seeing nothing.

After another two weeks and no further change, I realized the vet must have been mistaken. By this time I was sure that Bootsie was not pregnant.

Huh. I hadn't seen that coming.

By now she was pretty tame with me, although, like all ferals, at the slightest noise she would startle and run for cover. But when she felt safe? She lay in my lap, purring, and even allowed me to kiss her face. It was magical.

I realized she couldn't spend her life in that bathroom, so we got her spayed and I brought her into my room to live with the other kitties. She struggled there at first—it was much bigger, noisier, and had more places to hide—so she huddled at the back of the walk-in closet for days.

She eventually started interacting with the other cats, and even allowed me back onto her "ok list" again.

Then I moved out of our center and bought a house with my hubby in northern Virginia.

By this time I realized I was probably her mom. Ferals are hard to adopt out, and I felt like I'd be betraying her trust by giving her away to start over with another human, when she'd made so much progress with me.

We moved to a house in the woods along a river, and in the first week she escaped the house and was GONE. Oh, no! I felt so horrible, yet I told myself that she was better equipped than most to survive in the wild. It's where she was raised, and where she would have stayed had she not been successfully trapped in Pennsylvania.

I didn't see Bootsie for almost a year; by this time I believed she had died out there in those woods.

But then, in the dead of winter, Bootsie suddenly reappeared, slinking around outside in search of food. She was thin, but she was alive and I was ecstatic! I started feeding her, and finally, the day came when I successfully trapped her again and brought her back inside to start over.

Amazingly, she remembered me! Within only a half hour, she was sitting in my lap and biting me if I stopped petting her. She'd been desperately lonely outside, and seemed thrilled to be inside with me and the other kitties again.

Today Tootance doesn't even think of leaving the house. She remembers what it was like out in those cold woods alone, and wants no part of it. She's tubby, and soft, and lovely, and lays on her back like she hasn't a care in the world. One would never know from this photo that deep down she's still a feral kitty; she's learned to be part of a family, and I adore being her mom and sharing my life with her.

AND ALL THINGS NICE:
Cinnamon and Sugar

BY TAMIRA THAYNE

The Frigid Cold

I FELT SICK TO MY STOMACH. The wind chill measured 11 below zero, and to a chained-dog rescuer this meant only one thing: dogs were struggling to survive the harsh January temperatures while I lounged in the comparative lap of luxury. I had heat, after all.

And a warm bed. Not to mention rescue dogs, cats, kids, and a fiancé to snuggle with.

The guilt overwhelmed me, threatened to wrest the

last scraps of air from my lungs. I HAD to get up and DO SOMETHING. As much as I yearned to sprawl on the couch eating junk food and watching movies with my family—grateful to be inside on this frigid Sunday morning—my conscience wouldn't have it.

I hated to be cold for even the amount of time it took to sprint from the car to the house. To live outside in these harsh temps? Unimaginable.

Unacceptable.

Joe, my husband-to-be and the love of my short 46 years of life, was either still trying to win my heart or felt the pressure to do more himself. He quickly acquiesced to loading up straw, dog food, and water in his Durango and hitting the roads of rural Pennsylvania to see if we could ease the dogs' misery. And maybe save a life.

At least if I was taking action, I relieved my own nagging fears that I was little more than a party to the abuse—an uncaring and disinterested bystander of the daily cruelty that still goes on in backyards all across the United States. That's a tough pill to swallow.

My daughter Brynnan wanted to come visit the dogs too. At ten-years-old, she saw this as more of an adventure and less of a life and death operation, so she kept up a stream of inane chatter as we drove the country roads, scouring for dogs in trouble.

We left educational materials about chaining, plus straw, food, and water for a handful of freezing dogs. Joe was even on the receiving end of his first bite from a chained shepherd, missing the "get out of my territory" vibe the dog was throwing his way. Luckily he was wearing thick gloves and the bite didn't break the skin.

We had just hit the outskirts of the small town of Lilly when I saw HER.

She was a white ghost of a dog, huddled in her weathered plywood house against the swirling snow, face buried in her body in an attempt to keep what little warmth she had for herself. The opening of her shelter was too big, allowing the wind to whip right through and providing little to no protection from the elements. Its edges were rounded and gnawed, scarred by her attempts to stave off the all-too-frequent bouts of boredom and frantic neuroses that are typical of the chained dog.

"Stop!" I shouted. "Look at her! We have to stop."

Joe was understandably leery about engaging another dog so soon after surviving his first brush with chained-dog aggression, but he swung into the driveway of the ramshackle property anyway, his deliberately-loud exhaust (it's a man thing) announcing our arrival.

There was no sneaking around with that vehicle.

The white dog rose slowly and peered at us from the mouth of her barren shelter. Joe was not alone in his mistrust; her body language bespoke fear and an inability to conceive that a stranger could mean anything good for her. After all, when had this helpless creature—chained and abandoned to sub-zero temperatures by those who I'm sure would claim to "love" her—ever experienced a moment of actual compassionate care?

She was underweight, and medium in size, appearing to be some type of husky mix, giving her at least a measure of pelt thickness as protection from the cold. The same could not be said, unfortunately, for the short-haired boxer who shivered and barked for attention from her matching chain on the other side of the yard. She was skinny too.

Shit. Two dogs.

I sighed. "Let me go knock and see if they'll let us stuff the houses full of straw and give them the bones we brought. They definitely need them worse than any of the other dogs we've seen."

Brynnan and I trudged through the snow and hauled ourselves up the steps to the back door. We knocked repeatedly, but either the dog owners weren't home or they were avoiding the possibility of censorship by not answering.

Since there were no visible "No Trespassing" signs and no one to tell us otherwise, I took that as a clear signal to go ahead and offer the dogs our limited assistance. Make no mistake, these two dogs deserved to be removed from the situation and taken immediately into a home where they could be given warmth and loving kindness. It was painful for me to have to resist giving them this basic right.

The unbearable outdoor temperature and the body condition of these girls met no moral or humane standards. I, however, felt forced to stay well within the law if I wanted to avoid a second theft charge for helping a suffering dog. (Yes, I'd already been arrested and convicted of theft for aiding a chained dog who couldn't stand. I never regretted it—but I also wasn't eager to repeat that particular experience.)

I suspected that there were plenty of witnesses peeking out of neighboring windows even if these dog owners weren't home. People love a good gossip in these kinds of small towns, and I sensed rather than saw the eyes watching us.

So instead of giving the dogs what they truly needed and desired, we settled for giving both dogs large bones to gnaw on, as well as food and water which they immediately gobbled and slurped down. While I petted and loved on the dogs, Joe filled their houses with the straw we carried in the back of the Durango.

We'd done our best for them according to the law, but it wasn't enough. I despised a system that forced me to leave them in those unbearable conditions. It just wasn't right; I knew that in my gut and in every cell of my being.

The dogs were pitifully-thin and attention-starved, but also loving and without aggression. They shivered uncontrollably in the blowing snow and frigid wind, but jumped in excitement at the chance to experience even a moment of comfort and human companionship.

The white dog even did something I've never seen before or since: she "jumped rope" with her chain in her excitement to garner attention. She'd nimbly leap from side to side over the dragging links, her antics reminding me of playground days skipping rope with girls in my grade. I couldn't help but smile at how adorable she was, even during this, the grimmest of times.

I became determined to free these two girls from their chains. I left information for the owners, but promised the dogs I'd be back. It was a promise I would keep.

Round Number Two

It snowed all day Monday, but Joe had driven his four-wheel-drive back to Virginia where he lived and worked, so I was snowbound until the roads became more passable. By Wednesday it was clear enough to take the van out and make the forty-minute trip to Lilly to again attempt a meeting with the dog owners.

I knew without them willingly releasing the girls to rescue, I had little hope of bringing the dogs the freedom I'd promised.

This time I was alone, so I screwed up my courage to march once again to the door and knock. It's never easy for me to speak to people who chain their dogs. They quickly become defensive about their actions (which tells me they DO feel guilt), and there's a fine line one must walk between firmness and congeniality in order to affect chain-ge for these helpless dogs. Anger never got me anywhere.

I failed a lot.

Again, no one came to the door when I knocked. This time I left a note with my phone number and asked them to give me a call about the dogs. I then went out into the yard, petting and talked to the girls and once more providing them with food, water, and treats.

Just as I was walking back to my van, a woman opened the door on the back deck.

"What do you think you're doing with my dogs?" she yelled.

"Oh, hi!" I immediately affected a genial attitude in an attempt to diffuse the situation. "I was hoping we could speak about your dogs for a moment."

But she had herself already worked up, and screamed right over me as if I hadn't spoken. "I'm calling the police. Get off my property."

Well, that went south in a hurry.

I learned early on in dog rescue that if someone tells you to leave their property, DO IT and quick. The law in most states reads that once you are told to get off the property, either via a "No Trespassing" sign or a verbal or written warning from the owner, then you must leave immediately.

If you refuse to leave, or you come back without express permission, you can be charged with trespassing.

So I skedaddled…well, to be honest, I attempted to skedaddle. In reality, I got stuck in their driveway, instead. Awkward!

I wasn't winning any awards for my snow-driving abilities, admittedly, and my van was a bit cumbersome at best. So I was pretty scared I was gonna still be sitting there spinning and slogging when the police showed up and carted me off to jail. At the end of their 50-foot driveway one had to maneuver an immediate left up a small hill through a foot of snow, and I found I just couldn't get up the oomph to carry me out of there.

But that didn't stop me from trying. Screw that! I wasn't interested in being a sitting duck for the popo. That never ends well. (You'll never take me alive, coppers!)

Finally, on try number four-hundred-and-fifty-seven, I made it out onto the plowed roads without sirens screaming on my tail.

Whew! I was free.

Or so I thought.

Freedom Ain't So Free

I felt depressed that I hadn't been able to get anywhere on behalf of the little white husky and the boxer, and I couldn't get them out of my head. I hated that I'd made them a promise and had been unsuccessful in following through with it.

I knew logically that the dogs didn't understand the words

I'd said to them, and they were none the wiser that I'd made promises I couldn't keep. But for me, honoring my word was important. I'd let them down.

Plus, they were so adorable! And skinny…and needy.

And they needed me.

That weekend, I was visiting Joe at his place in Virginia when my cell phone rang. The man on the other end identified himself as a Pennsylvania State Police Officer, and my first thought was, "Oh, crap, here we go!"

"Ma'am, were you at this residence in Lilly, PA on two different occasions in the past week?"

"Yes, yes I was," I told him, attempting to stay very matter-of-fact. "My organization was doing welfare checks on chained dogs due to the bitter cold and sub-zero wind-chills—without help dogs were sure to die that day. No dogs anywhere in the state should have been left out to fend for themselves in that weather. We visited some of the dogs in the area and offered our services."

"I understand that, but it doesn't give you the right to trespass."

"On the contrary, sir, I never trespassed. I know the law. There were no signs on the property and no one answered the door. Sunday we left the dogs food, water, and straw without seeing or speaking to a single soul. As I was very concerned about the weight and health of those two dogs, I went back Wednesday to speak to someone; yet still there was no answer when I knocked. When the woman came out and told me to leave, I immediately did as she asked…that is, as soon as I could get out of her driveway."

He obviously didn't believe me. "That's not what the dog owner tells me. She says they told you to leave Sunday and not come back, and yet you came back again on Wednesday without their permission. That's defiant trespass, so I'm going to have to cite you."

By now I *was* feeling kinda defiant, now that he mentioned it. "Well, that's definitely not true, and I have a witness and videotape to prove it. Doesn't it matter that she's lying?"

"Ma'am, that you can take up with the magistrate."

Going Public with the Case

I hoped it would blow over and they would threaten to charge me but go along their merry way once he realized I had evidence to back up my story, but it wasn't to be the case.

After I received my court summons in the mail, I went public with my side of the story, posting videos and photos of the condition of the dogs and the steps we'd taken to help them. Citizens across the nation were appalled both by the condition of the dogs—the boxer's ribs and spine were very clearly showing as she gobbled her food—and by the fact that those who step up to help the suffering are attacked, while those who abuse get away with it time and again.

Mid-February found us at our hearing date before the magistrate in Lilly, Pennsylvania. The dog owners blatantly lied on the stand, claiming that they had told us to leave the property on Sunday and I came back Wednesday in violation of the trespass law. The cop I had spoken to was acting as attorney for their side—but he had not been there and only had their word to go by.

Both Joe and I testified that the temperatures had been

single digits with sub-zero wind chills, the dogs were under-weight and had no food or water, the shelter was inadequate, and we hadn't seen or spoken to a single soul there on that cold January day.

When Krystal—the female half of the dog owners who'd yelled at me that Wednesday—was on the stand Joe whispered to me, "Ask her what color and kind of vehicle we were driving on Sunday."

I'm not an attorney, I just played one in this court case, so I was open to and recognized a genius strategy when I saw one. I asked her the trick question.

Her response? "You were driving a tan van."

I circled for the kill. "Are you SURE we were in a tan van on Sunday when you first told us to leave the property?"

"Yes, I'm sure."

Bingo! We had them dead to rights now.

Or, once again, so I thought.

We immediately (and with a certain smugness, to be sure) produced video from that Sunday which clearly showed Joe's blue Durango as the vehicle we drove to the location and pulled our supplies from. It also showed us knocking on the door and no one answering before we provided aid to the dogs.

Alas, it seems these genius strategies play well on TV when the judges know they've been lied to and acknowledge real evidence when they see it. But apparently magistrates in Pennsylvania aren't required to be actual lawyers, and therefore are less likely to abide by the letter of the law when it suits them to ignore it. This guy was no lawyer.

He didn't care that we had proven her to be lying; he claimed we could have doctored the video, instead.

He was more concerned about the fact that one of my supporters had sent him a letter about the case. Which pissed him off. Ouch. I've learned the hard way that judges don't like citizens writing them letters; it usually ends badly for the defendant. In this case, me.

So he found me guilty.

We had driven Joe's Durango to the hearing, and after that crushing defeat, I was glad we had. When we went out into the parking lot, Joe walked up to the officer and simply nodded toward his Durango, as if to say, "There it is. Who's lying now?"

The officer simply nodded in return and walked away.

An Appeal for Justice

We appealed the conviction and this automatically sent my case out of the magistrate's office (thank Dog) and before a "real" judge in Cambria County, Pennsylvania.

This time I realized I had to hire an attorney if I was going to play with the big boys. I got incredibly lucky that I'd met a wonderful attorney named Rick who was working a dog hoarding and chaining case in northern Pennsylvania. He was a former prosecutor, and was nearing retirement. He wanted to use what was left of his career to make a few differences for the downtrodden, and so he took my case, only charging us for his mileage and hotel stay.

I've dealt with my share of bad attorneys since starting to help chained dogs, and most have made me think I could do a better job myself. (And we've all seen how well THAT goes.) This was not the case with Rick. He was kind, intelligent, and completely on top of the situation from the second he walked into the courthouse.

We had audiotaped the first court hearing, planning to use that as evidence of their perjury in the second. However, unbeknownst to us at the time, the taping had failed and was a garbled mess. We would be left without that crucial piece of evidence. Frustrating.

On the bright side, we realized that although WE knew that our audiotape had failed, the false accusers wouldn't know that until they hit the courtroom. They would be extra nervous about the appeal hearing because they knew what proof we held, both in our video from that Sunday and from—as far as they knew—the taping of their lies. They were looking at evidence of perjury whether they stuck to their story or changed it at the higher court level.

I was incredibly stressed about the hearing, and waited anxiously for the accusers to show up that May morning at the county courthouse to start the next round of this dog and pony show. The state policeman was there, as expected, but the dog owners simply NEVER SHOWED UP!

They never showed up.

The relief was overwhelming.

The judge then—because the Commonwealth's case against me no longer had any evidence—threw out the trespassing charge and I was free to go.

After he lectured me, of course, on why I needed to stay off other people's property.

Yes, Judge. Whatever you say, Judge.

To be clear, I considered the dogs my clients, not the judge or the dogs' owners. I highly doubted the husky and the boxer would have been in agreement with any lecture that withheld the lifesaving straw, food, and water from them on that cold January day. Therefore, as I saw it, it was my duty to let that lecture go in one ear and out the other.

I was finally free of the court case.

Not Everyone is Free

Of course, the dogs were still not free, and it was five months since I'd first laid eyes on them that frigid January day.

Ironically, the owners had sought to imprison me in much the same way they had imprisoned their dogs...without a care about truth, right and wrong, and moral actions and reactions. I couldn't help but believe it was my empathy for their dogs (which, by default, pointed out their lack of empathy) that lead them to lash out.

People will never like us standing up against their obvious cruelty and neglect, but we should continue to be a voice for those who have none anyway. We're all they've got.

I thought of the girls often, but there was nothing further I could legally do about their living situation. I knew I was not welcome to visit again, and I told myself repeatedly that I had to let it go.

I had to content myself with liberating the dogs I COULD save, and try not to beat myself up too badly over the ones I couldn't.

Who Believes in Miracles?

Then a miracle occurred.

Only three weeks later, in early June, I got a call on my cell phone from Jason Cann, the male half of the dog-owning duo. I didn't pick up the phone as the number was not one I recognized, but he left a message asking me to call him back, that the family wanted to give up the dogs to my rescue organization.

What?!?!

I was flabbergasted, flummoxed, flea-ridden. OK, maybe I wasn't flea-ridden, but I couldn't think of another "fl" word. I was actually DUBIOUS. (The dogs were probably flea-ridden.)

I honestly couldn't—and didn't—believe he was telling me the truth. I thought it was a trick for them to lure me back onto their property to have me arrested again.

Hell, no. Fool me once...

But I had to call Jason back. If there was ANY chance this was a legitimate offer to free these girls, I had to take it. I was courteous on the phone, but understandably wary.

"Hi, Jason, this is Tamira Thayne. I got your message. Are you really willing to let the girls go to rescue? I have to admit, I'm a bit skeptical given all that has happened since January."

"Yeah, we thought about it a lot; because of your campaign, people from all over the U.S. wrote us letters about our dogs. We decided we wanted to be the people who made a difference in our dogs' lives, and not the ones who kept them in a bad situation because of our pride. Would you still be willing to take them into your rescue and find them good homes?"

Thrilled wouldn't exactly cover my level of excitement. Tears, happy tears, threatened, but I tamped my joy down until I got off the phone, keeping things as matter-of-fact as possible under the circumstances. "Of course I'll take them!

I won't come on your property, though, for obvious reasons; I have to protect myself. But I'll gladly meet you at a public place, and we can do the exchange there."

We arranged to meet the next evening at a park in Lilly, Pennsylvania, not far from their home. When I arrived, as promised, Jason and his son were already there waiting with the two dogs. The family must not have owned leashes, because the dogs were still on their chains, dragging the menfolk around the parking lot behind them in their excitement at being anywhere but their stifling back yard.

To say the exchange was awkward would have been putting it mildly, but I did my best to be kind. I respected that in the end they had made the right decision, and any time someone makes an effort to make amends, my attitude toward them immediately softens.

The dogs were a better weight than they'd been in January, and were straining at the ends of their "leash-chains" to get to me for a sniff and a quick hello. I chose to save my exuberance at their release for when we got home, giving them both a brief petting session, but I couldn't help but smile knowing that I'd been able to keep my promise to the girls after all.

Jason signed the paperwork releasing the dogs to my organization, and helped me corral them and get them into the back of the van—newly-freed chained dogs are nothing if not exuberant!

As we pulled away, I gave him and his son a respectful wave and nod of appreciation, then looked in the rearview mirror to where the dogs were gated off in the back of the vehicle. The girls had their noses plastered to the windows, eagerly taking in the new sights, smells, and sounds of a world heretofore unseen. Their naïve innocence grabbed my heart and squeezed.

And then, and only then, I allowed myself a bit of a cry.

We'd done it! They were free.

In that moment I made the girls another promise, one I knew I could keep: that they'd never see the end of a chain again.

Epilogue: Within the week both girls got the vet care they needed through my organization in order to be put up for adoption to new—INSIDE ONLY!—homes. We re-named them Sugar (the husky) and Cinnamon (the boxer), because for me their release was so sweet, their dispositions so loving, they were the epitome of "Sugar and Spice and All Things Nice".

Cinnamon quickly found a home, and was such an easy-going dog she immediately settled in and made herself part of the family.

Sugar was with me for foster care and training a while longer; she was more fearful of humans, and not every home understands the needs of a shy dog. But when she did finally find her family, she was immense-ly treasured by them; they regularly sent photos and updates of her progress from shy girl to what they described as a silly and adorable mischief-maker.

I did my best to put the ugliness of the previous six months behind me and focus on the end result: the freedom I'd obtained for two suffering dogs.

And all things nice, indeed.

જ

Tamira Thayne is the author of *The Wrath of Dog, The King's Tether, Foster Doggie Insanity,* and *Capitol in Chains,* and the co-editor of *Unchain My Heart* and *Rescue Smiles.*

Tamira pioneered the anti-tethering movement in America, forming and leading the nonprofit Dogs Deserve Better for 13 years; her swan song culminated in the purchase and transformation of Michael Vick's dogfighting compound to a chained-dog rescue and rehabilitation center.

Finding Sanctuary:
Von Truman

by Rachel Ogden

It was the end of February when I took on what I initially hoped would be a simple rescue mission to save a sweet bare-eyed cockatoo that was posted on Craigslist. The ad pictured a little white bird with delicate-looking blue skin around his eyes, stuck in a disturbingly small cage.

Along with the photo was a short description, noting the death of a family member as the reason for selling him. Over the next few days, I texted with the person who posted the ad, pleading with her to surrender the bird to a wonderful cockatoo sanctuary I knew about in Maryland. It seemed the only responses I was receiving mentioned money; obviously wanting the best for this bird was not of importance to this person.

I told her that I would try to raise money to get the cockatoo into rescue. She told me if I had the money to buy him I could come get him, but she wasn't going to just give him up to any rescue organization.

From the responses, I began to wonder if it was some sort of scam—which is not uncommon on Craigslist and other online selling platforms. I debated with myself and friends about whether or not we should even pay to rescue an animal. I'm a firm believer in never buying animals from pet stores or breeders so as not to support an industry that views non-humans as "products."

After discussing the bird's plight in-depth with family, friends, and fellow Facebook rescuers, I decided that this sort of situation would be more acceptable than supporting the "pet" industry. If not a scam, this would be a legitimate rescue that would change the bird's life for the better and not condemn any other animals in the process.

I spent several days texting back and forth with the woman who had the cockatoo, and my anxiety was through the roof at my lack of progress in freeing the bird. One of the last texts I received from her told me to stop "harassing" her, even though I had only offered to help get him to the sanctuary if she agreed to relinquish him.

While I was still feeling very uneasy about the whole situation, I couldn't stop thinking about the little guy and his beautiful eyes. Intent upon saving this one, I asked my friend, Carl, to text the person simply stating he had cash and wanted to pick up the bird. Carl got an immediate response when he mentioned he had the money, and the meeting was set. Carl said he would go with me to investigate.

During the hour-and-a-half drive to get the cockatoo, my stomach was in knots. What if this was a scam? What if the person was really a breeder and we could hear the squawks of birds they were using for breeding? The "what-if" scenarios running through my mind were endless. Carl, on the other hand, was optimistic and said we'd play it by ear once we got there.

When we arrived at the house I felt queasy. Carl rang the doorbell. My ears picked up several timid, lonely cockatoo calls. His calls pulled at my heart, and I couldn't wait to meet him. The fact that I only heard him was a good sign.

No other birds. This wasn't a breeder.

Luckily for us and the bird, there was no scam. There was only one sweet boy existing in a tiny cage all by himself—alone more than 23 hours a day since the woman who kept him died at the end of January. When I saw the cage sitting on top of a stand in the kitchen, my heart sank.

I had hoped the cage in the photos was some sort of travel cage, but it wasn't; it was the tiny, rusty cage this boy had lived in since 2009. The cage the woman who was selling him described as "not that small though" when I commented about how I hated to see him in such a small cage. There were no toys in the cage. None. There was only one single dirty plastic dowel for him to perch on.

The bottom of the cage was filthy. His water bowl was filled with grime and some sort of bright red residue filled the corners. He was being fed seeds and dried corn, the worst kinds of food for a parrot who would eat a fresh, var-

Who Chains You Books

ied diet in the wild. His basic needs weren't even being met. I felt even sicker.

As soon as his beautiful blue-rimmed eyes saw us walk into the dimly lit home, he became very excited. The crest feathers on his head raised high. He made soft sounds and leaned towards us. This little guy was starved for attention, longing for contact, for love.

However, when we slowly approached the cage, he flinched. We softly reassured him and soon he welcomed pets on his head through the cruddy cage bars. The woman let us see his paperwork showing he had been purchased from Canary Bird Farm in New Jersey, a store that had thankfully gone out of business. She offered us a dusty bag of food, sold by the same store and tagged as "Parrot Mix Large".

Later, when disposing of the food, I found it infested with small black bugs, some alive, some dead, and maggots. Yuk!

We handed over the $400—the price the woman decided his freedom was worth—and with very few questions or interaction with the woman, we were invited to take both him and his tiny cage. Carl loaded the cage into the car as the woman spoke with me. I never let on that I was the person who had been texting her asking her to do the right thing for the bird. I didn't want to risk her turning us away because she thought I had bothered her with my texts.

As the woman spoke she had tears in her eyes. I thought I was seeing things at first. Why was she crying? The woman said that when she visited her aunt in the past, it seemed her aunt really loved the bird. The woman cried saying goodbye to him, something I still don't understand to this day. This is someone who I had begged to surrender the bird, a bird

125

who was in desperate need of proper care, to a sanctuary and she chose to tell me to stop "harassing" her. Maybe she cried because she felt guilty? I'll never know.

I dropped Carl off, thanking him profusely for his help in freeing the cockatoo from his sub-par living conditions, and picked up my other friend Bobby, who had pledged to make the two-hour trip to the sanctuary in Maryland with me. Before the drive, I was able to open the cage and interact with the sweet, feathered boy I'd been worried sick about for days.

It's quite possible that he had never seen the cage door swing that wide open before. His eyes widened in amazement. He immediately grabbed my hand and pulled it towards him, rubbing his beak and head sweetly against me. He'd been craving touch. As far as I knew, he had never been let out of his tiny cage. Ever. I cried and told him I was so sorry.

During the car ride he was curious and seemed to enjoy all of the sights, except for flashing lights, which scared him. We played different kinds of music for him, and his favorite seemed to be rap—with Bobby creating a special personalized freestyle all about him—and I'd swear he appreciated even my off-key singing (well, someone has to!), and he actually bobbed his head a few times.

Christi, the founder and director of The Icarus Cockatoo Sanctuary, had replied enthusiastically to an email I sent after finding the Craigslist ad, saying she would absolutely accept the little cockatoo. Christi had texted me all day, anxiously awaiting updates about her new resident. When we arrived at the sanctuary, Christi welcomed all of us with open arms. She had an awesome quarantine area set up with a huge cage, tons of toys, full spectrum lighting, and yummy food.

On the way there, I had tried feeding the sweet guy pieces of apple and spaghetti but he didn't seem to know what they were. When I presented the apple piece, he gently rubbed the side of his face against it. At the sanctuary, all of the parrots are given a variety of fresh foods every day so he will be introduced to new foods and will get plenty of his favorites.

It took awhile to transfer him to the larger cage, as he was focused on collecting head scratches and testing out his beak on our fingers. Once he was safely in his new and greatly enlarged home, he began exuberantly climbing around and checking everything out.

Earlier in the day we'd been told that all he'd ever been called was "pretty bird". While that is a nice term of endearment, it's not a name. I decided this boy needed a name that described his spirit and will to live even though he was trapped in a tiny prison. I looked up names that meant "hope". I found two names and loved them both.

I named him Von Truman. Turns out Truman means something along the lines of "faithful", but it's still a name that suits him well. He could be called Von or Truman for short. He seemed to approve of both, or maybe he just liked when I repeated them in a sing-songy voice.

Although The Icarus Cockatoo Sanctuary is amazing and Christi is a wonderful person, I had such a hard time leaving the little man. I had already grown so attached through the week's ordeal, and I knew I'd fallen hard for him; but I also understood he was in the good hands of an expert, and I needn't worry about him.

Before we left, I looked into his beautiful eyes and again

saw his loneliness and longing for affection. But shining beyond that was the continued hope that had kept him strong and healthy through the many sad years; hope for a better future, the future he deserved and the future he could now have. I kissed his beak and reminded him that he was safe.

Update: As I write this story, Von Truman is doing extremely well at The Icarus Cockatoo Sanctuary. Surprisingly, all of his bloodwork came back within normal range, so this little survivor managed to stay fairly healthy despite his less than ideal conditions. Christi keeps me informed about all the new foods he is trying, and what he enjoys the best. He is a fan of peas and pistachios, but apparently doesn't care too much for carrots.

I feel so grateful to everyone who helped me raise the funds to purchase his freedom and a brighter future. Live long and prosper, Von Truman!

༂ఔ

Rachel Ogden has been vegan and a social justice activist for about a decade. Rachel's work includes protesting against breeders, breeding mills, and pet stores, with a special focus on the exploitation of parrots; organizing the Break Frame's campaign against the transportation sector of the animal experimentation industry; teaching children about animal liberation using stories, art, and music; and, of course, rescuing non-human animals.

A degree in elementary education and psychology has led Rachel to act in various social service positions. Rachel is also an artist who uses her art to educate about the plight of animals and to implore people to take action for the innocent.

No More Chains:
Gator

by Melody Whitworth

We were having a gorgeous fall here in Columbia, Missouri, and multiple calls were coming into our rescue group with regards to a yellow lab-shepherd mix that was living out on a trolley cable that ran from a house to a big oak tree. This boy had a large three-sided wooden box, his only shelter, with an old couch cushion in the yard for him to lay on.

One day, when his frustration with being alone and confined finally got the best of him, he ripped the cushion into a million pieces. Foam pieces from the cushion coated the front yard, resembling a snow fall. People would slow down to observe this beautiful boy, and often threw him bread or dog treats from their car windows. Some would stop and talk baby talk to him, which simply made him crazy with excitement.

After multiple complaints filled my voicemail and e-mail, I drove by one morning to see the poor boy for myself. There were cars in the driveway, so I stopped and talked to some college-age kids that answered the door. They assured me that they did not like that the dog, named Teddy, was out on this cable all day, every day. They said they were living with an uncle, and that Teddy was his dog. Because Teddy didn't have any manners in the house (due to lack of proper training, of course), out into the yard he went.

We discussed options our organization could provide for Teddy, such as appropriate training and even re-homing him. The kids were very receptive and said they would talk to their uncle about better options for Teddy.

When I followed up a few days later, the uncle was not willing to allow my rescue group to re-home Teddy. He stated that Teddy was a great dog and that he "loved" him; he felt Teddy was just fine the way he was. The college kids who lived there told me that Teddy would soon be going to the vet to get updated on his vaccinations as requested by Animal Control.

At that same time, they reported a dog a couple of houses down from them, telling me "There's a dog down the street that REALLY needs your help." They walked me to the back of their yard where we could peek through the trees, and there we saw a very thin, red-coated dog, tied to a building with barely any room to turn around. I told them to let me know how they made out at the vet's office, and I was off to the house with the tied red dog.

The house I approached was a cute little cottage with a pleasant front porch. Children's bicycles lined the sidewalk leading up to the front door. I knocked and was greeted by a woman who was probably in her mid-30's, but who looked much older due to the smoke from the cigarette that hung from her mouth.

I politely said "hello," introduced myself, and told her that some neighbors were concerned about the dog in the backyard. I asked if she needed any food or help for him. She flung open the door, excited at the mention of "free food." Then she stepped out onto the porch and explained that she could not afford food for him; that she had gone to the local humane society but had been denied donations of food because the dog was not vaccinated.

She claimed she could not afford to have him vaccinated, and so the poor dog was living off table scraps. I quickly went to my truck and took out a 40-pound bag of food, gave it to her with no strings attached, and then asked if I could meet the dog.

It was yet another beautiful fall day in mid-Missouri, so getting to the backyard was an easy walk, but when I turned around the back corner of the house, I stopped dead in my tracks and gasped for breath. There he was, starving and banged up, with only a make-shift box covered in black plastic serving as his shelter.

At first I was speechless, but I quickly shook it off, saying, "What a beautiful dog, what's his name?" The women replied, "Name's Gator. I rescued him from an abusive situation."

My first thought was, "If this was not the most abusive situation that poor dog had suffered through, I didn't even want to know where he'd come from." I told her that even though we were having beautiful weather right now, a storm was coming and the weather would soon be turning very cold; this poor dog needed some shelter, and he needed it now.

She was very receptive to anything that I could do for her so I made arrangements to come back the next morning.

I was numb after leaving the property. After all of the situations I'd seen—chained dog after chained dog—this one had rattled me and gotten under my skin like no other. Not only was Gator on a very short rope, he had basically no shelter, he was skin and bones, and he looked like he had been tormented and tortured.

The building he was tied to housed multiple cats, and the cats would run in and out the door just past his nose, causing him to react and give chase, only to have his neck snapped back each time he reached the end of his three-foot rope. It was more than heartbreaking; it was gut-wrenching, and my heart and my stomach ached for this poor dog.

I stopped wallowing in my sadness and got busy preparing for the next day. A dog house, a bale of straw, flea and tick medications, a giant bone, and more food and treats were loaded up for delivery. I spent a very restless night, not only due to thoughts of Gator and the conditions we'd found him in, but also because thunderstorms had moved in and it poured all night.

Horrific booms of thunder and flashes of lightning filled the sky, and we could only imagine what Gator and all of the other dogs forced to live outside were experiencing: fear, anxiety, wet and cold conditions, and no way to escape the elements. How people can lay comfy in their beds while the

Who Chains You Books

dogs are suffering out there is something I will never comprehend.

The next morning I was excited to go back and visit
Gator, give him his supplies, and hopefully bring him a bit of
relief. It was still pouring rain. I knocked on the front door
of the charming little house and was once again welcomed
in with our supplies. Multiple family members followed us
to the back where Gator was imprisoned. It was windy, cold,
sopping wet, and generally miserable out.

Gator's box had collapsed due to the rain, and he paced
back and forth, cowering, showing us he meant no harm
and begging for us to help him. We quickly unloaded the
doghouse, and even as we were filling it with straw, Gator
was burrowing in before we could reattach the top, desperate to get some relief from the cold and rain. We gave him
the biggest bone we could find from the farm store and he
chewed on it like he had never had a bone in his life. He
probably hadn't.

While other volunteers put Gator's doghouse together
and spread straw on the ground to cover the mud, I talked
to the owner of the house and mother of the children that
joined us in the backyard. I thanked her for "rescuing" him
from an abusive situation but explained that being tied to a
building 24/7 is no life for a dog, and that we could find him
a better home if she would allow us to.

Once again, she was receptive to our ideas, and agreed to
legally transfer him to our rescue, recognizing that she could
not properly take care of him. We always carry surrender
forms with us, so we were able to quickly pull one out and
have her sign the paperwork on the spot. We knew we would
be planting the seed for him to be surrendered and turned

over to our organization that day, but we were surprised and relieved when it went so easily.

We were ready to put a slip lead around Gator to remove him from his hellish existence in that mud pit when a young woman approached us and asked, "What's he worth to you?"

I stopped what I was doing, turned to her, and simply said, "What do you mean?"

"Well, if you are taking our dog and you get money for him, he must be worth something to you," she responded.

I explained that our group is an all-volunteer group, and no members of Unchained Melodies Dog Rescue receive compensation from the donations given by our supporters. I also explained that the vetting that Gator needed would well exceed the money that we would receive for his adoption fee. I spelled it out for her, letting her know that his neuter alone would be around $100, but that we would have to work hard to raise the funds needed for his veterinary care.

I also told her that we never, ever pay for a dog that we help. She then took a big drag of her cigarette, looked up at me with discerning eyes, and said, "Do you neuter boy-friends?"

The tension had now dissipated from the air. I cheekily replied, "Yes, ma'am! Put him in the truck and we will take him with us to the clinic right now." We both laughed and she walked over to Gator to say her goodbyes.

Gator was now free!

He was a muddy mess, but we quickly got him bathed, gave him a big bowl of fresh food which he gobbled down, and the next day he went to the vet to get the works.

Gator had a long road ahead of him. He suffered from extreme separation anxiety. Gator worked with a trainer and had a very dedicated foster home, but Gator's issues were so bad that when he was crated, he would poop, pee, and destroy the crate in a frenzy to get out. If not crated, he would tear blinds and curtains from the windows, rip up carpet, and destroy anything in his path. Months passed and the work continued. Gator went to multiple events and always charmed people, but when we would discuss his separation anxiety issues the interest would diminish and people would walk away.

Finally, a local family who follows our social media and are longtime supporters of our work for chained dogs fell in love with Gator's pictures, and his story pulled at their heart strings. The transition for Gator would be a difficult one, but this family had someone home most of the time, and they were dedicated and devoted to helping him. Gator was a challenge for sure! He would tear through their house, jump the fence, and drag his people down the sidewalk when they took him for a walk.

He even broke a thousand dollar antique lamp. Yikes!

With weeks of training, understanding, and a bond that grew stronger every day, Gator started settling into his new life, and was well on his way to becoming a permanent member of the family.

Today, Gator is loved unconditionally. He still poses a challenge when strangers come to the home or he is left alone for any length of time—but his family takes it in stride, and always teases that Gator can do no wrong.

We continue to receive updates on him, and offer help with old and new issues that arise with Gator, who will always be mentally damaged from his years of neglect and abuse. But even with his anxiety and possessive tendencies, he is a loving, loyal dog.

A strong bond has been made, not only with Gator and his forever family, but with members of the community who know of Gator and his story. Gator has officially become the poster dog for chained dogs in the Columbia area, and is a bit of a celebrity for all he's gone through to become a loving family member.

As for the yellow lab named Teddy that led us to Gator? The local shelter called and told us he'd been dropped off there by the college kids I'd spoken to at the home. The kids tipped off the shelter staff that we had stopped by offering help, hoping they would contact us. So we picked up Teddy from the shelter, too, got him into our foster care program, and are happy to report that he now has a loving, forever home of his own.

Yes, our rescue dogs are a lot of work, but there's no greater feeling than pulling dogs off the cruel chain and watching them blossom into the happy creatures they were always meant to be. I feel blessed to take part in so many happy endings with Unchained Melodies Dog Rescue, and grateful to all those who make our efforts possible.

࿊

Melody Whitworth, upon relocating from Florida to Columbia, Missouri, started seeing chained dog after chained dog after chained dog, a concept that she could not accept or ignore. After reaching out to local authorities and rescue groups, she learned there was no help or hope for chained dogs in her area.

Melody insisted and persisted in finding help for these poor souls and formed a tutelage relationship with Tamira Thayne, who spear-headed the anti-chaining movement across the country.

Melody is now the President/Director of Unchained Melodies Dog Rescue, whose mission is to rescue, rehabilitate and rehome the chained, penned, abused and neglected back yard dog. Visit unchainedmelodies. org to learn more about this fast growing, all volunteer organization and how you can support them and their mission.

THE CHURCH LADIES:
Lonestar and Tejas

BY JOE MARINGO

TODAY'S LIFE IS FULL OF SOCIAL MEDIA; cell phones and websites like Facebook are the norm. It's hard to remember a time when we just sent emails back and forth and made good old-fashioned phone calls. That was how things were early in my rescue career—I would make sure to check my emails several times a day to see if there was any important news or emergencies in the process of happening.

That was exactly the catalyst for the wonderful and amazing chain of events that awaited me when I jumped into my e-mail to check my messages one night in early July.

I can still clearly remember it being later at night, after dark. I was not in the habit of checking things right before bed, but for some reason that night I did. One of the first emails that came up had been forwarded dozens of times before coming to me, and had traveled all over the country for weeks. It had come all the way from Cedar Creek, Texas.

The title caught me a little off guard, and at the same time it drew me in to take a closer look. ARE YOU MY DADDY? Was the subject line, and it ended up being a Craigslist posting, seemingly listed by a Labrador puppy who, being very smart like all labs, must have learned how to type and operate a computer. The following is the actual listing that I received:

Are you my Daddy?..or Mommy? (Cedar Creek Lake)

I'm writing this for me and my mommy. Right now we are living in a deserted church. Well, guess it's not deserted, totally, 'cause we live there. It's a really neat place, we just jump through the windows, and there are no doors. Yesterday, my mommy found an old quilt in the back of the church and she drug it up to the front, and now we have a bed. This lady brings us food and water every day. At first we were scared of her, but now we run and jump all over her. Today my mommy showed me how to jump straight up in the air...at least two feet high. The lady said she wished she could take us home, but she already has two dogs and her dogs told her that "Two was company, three was a crowd."

I'm not gonna dwell on how hard we've had it, cause I think we really have, but I'm not gonna let that get me down. I am happy and friendly. I think it has been harder on my mommy. I don't remember, but think I must have had some brothers or sister, but guess they weren't as strong as me, cause they didn't make it. Mommy has a sore on her neck that looks like she was tied up and maybe hurt, but she doesn't talk about it, so I'm not sure what happened.

But she's happy too, did I tell you she can do the high jump?

Someone said I was a black lab. Mommy never mentions my daddy, but he must have looked like us, cause I am the spitting image of my mommy. Our new friend checked with a safe place to take us, but they told her that black dogs are hard to adopt, and if we didn't get a new home real quick-like we would be taking a verrrry long nap. There are way too many things to do for long naps. Leaves to chase, papers to rip, water to splash. Mommy and I love to run round and round the church. She is a great mommy and loves to play with me.

Sometimes the lady calls us Saint and Sinner (she said most all churches have those) and today she called Mommy Tigger.

You really don't have to call us anything, we'll love you anyway.

Mommy has the kindest eyes you will ever see...me... well, mine just look kinda mischievous!

There wouldn't be any rehoming fee...maybe a rechurching. And we would be willing to be baptized, dipped or sprinkled into any other faith.

You think about it...okay?? If you live on the lake and I could go swimming every day....now I'm dreaming. I'm a big girl now and I don't HAVE to go with my mommy, but if your heart is big 'nuff for me, maybe you could squeeze her in too??

Tell our friend all about you, cause she really wants us to find someone special. (We don't have a phone or internet, so you have to talk with her.)

Here are some pictures...not my best pose, but in this heat no one's hair looks good!

See ya' soon!

After reading the posting, I was in tears, and I have to admit that even now, almost 10 years later, tears still well up in my eyes when I read it again. Had it been like most postings that just said "FREE DOGS, NO CHARGE" I would probably not have been so touched—but luckily for those girls, it wasn't.

I did some backtracking and found the name and number to contact the original poster of the listing. Then the story gets even more incredible. I spoke to Donita on the phone that same night. She was an interior decorator, and she would often just drive through the countryside of rural Texas, looking for unwanted and abandoned items that she could repurpose for clients who wanted a touch of country in their expensive homes.

On one of her trips she came upon a long-abandoned church, and upon investigating further, came across the two dogs that we later started calling "the church ladies." No one knew how long the dogs had been living there, but there was no real food except what they could find lying on the rural road, and even worse, in the 110-degree Texas summer heat. There was no water anywhere nearby either. The Momma dog was in severe distress when she found her, and we later discussed that she'd been easily within hours of passing away. Having had a litter of pups under those serious conditions had ravaged her body.

A healthy lab of her frame size should easily weigh 60-plus pounds, but this poor dog was a lot closer to just 20 pounds. She had gotten to the point where she would not get up and move, and while the puppy came running out to see who had come to visit, Momma just lay on the old mattress on the church altar, and did not even stir when their savior came inside. She actually thought Momma had passed away until she walked right up to her and saw the faintest tail wag. This is the true sign of the lab; despite all that humans have thrown at them, if there is life left in them, they will wag their tails because they are ever happy to please.

Donita was horrified at the conditions, and decided right then and there she would do something about it. Having dogs of her own, she knew she could not bring the two of them home, but she could bring them food and water twice a day. You may not think that is much, but when you consider that Donita lived 45 miles away, that meant she was driving 180 miles a day just to bring food and water to a couple of stray dogs.

Again, I was in tears just listening to the story, and the love she had grown in her heart for these precious lives. She continued this ritual for weeks while she tried everything she could think of to find help for the girls. She feared the local shelters would put the dogs down for lack of room and adopters, and she could not find any friends or family who had any interest in taking them.

She even posted flyers offering the dogs for adoption, but

nothing worked. Meanwhile, Donita continued bringing necessities to the dogs, and watched them start to recover their health and grow stronger. Momma was now gaining weight, and would run to meet her when she pulled in. The danger now was that the dogs would wander out in search of food and things to do, and would often cross the road in front of the church. It was a dangerous road on a blind curve with a 70 mile per hour speed limit. Donita dreaded the thought that she had saved these lost souls only to lose one or both of them to a speeding car.

Something had to be done, and quickly. That is when she got the idea of posting on Craigslist from the point of view of the puppy, and that is where I came into the story.

At this point, I was all in for helping these dogs, and had already fallen for them through Donita's tale. I told her I would drive from Pennsylvania to Texas sometime within the next week, and would bring both girls back with me. How could I even consider splitting them up after all they had been through? Now it was Donita's turn to be in tears, and she thanked me profusely for my kindness, to both her and the dogs. To this day, I wonder who could have said no after reading that listing?

We hung up and I turned off the computer and went to bed; but I could not sleep.

I had my wife read the listing the next day, and after reading it she only asked me two questions; "When are you leaving," and "How long will you be gone?"

Just 24 hours later I was on my way to Texas, with my constant companion Bubba by my side. Bubba went everywhere I went, as he was a great ambassador for the Labrador breed. At 90 pounds he was a stunning yellow boy, and always drew a lot of attention wherever we went. It was a long trip at 1150 miles each way, but I knew I had to do all I could to get there before something horrible happened. We drove nonstop through the night, and then early the next morning, I received wonderful news; Donita had been able to find someone local willing to board the girls and keep them safe until I arrived.

That was a relief. They were no longer at the church, but I still wanted to see the place where they had spent so much time.

We decided to just meet at the church when I got into the area, so I could see it before picking up the dogs. It was obvious that it had been empty for a very long time. There were piles of garbage all the way around it, and inside was trashed as well. Empty beer cans filled the parking lot, and there were signs that there had been a lot of people around who most likely were not so friendly to helpless animals. I was surprised the poor things had survived life in that hellhole.

The roof was open to the sky in places, the doors and windows were long gone, and weeds were growing through the openings. The old mattress where the girls had spent so many days and nights was still on the altar. It was a truly depressing sight, but knowing that they had survived and were now going to have a better life made it not seem quite so bad. I hugged Donita and thanked her for caring when so many others would have just said, "Oh well, they're just dogs." Then we said our goodbyes.

I drove the 30 miles to the boarding facility quickly because I wanted to meet my new girls. It was sometime along that drive that I decided they needed names, real names, Texas names. Two names popped into my mind.

Momma would now be called Lonestar, and her last lucky puppy would be named Tejas. A short time later, I met the girls and called them by their new forever names for the first time.

Little Tejas was friendly and outgoing. She would run and jump and bounce over her mom from side to side, just like the little dog on the Saturday morning cartoons used to do. Lonestar was a different story. She was not aggressive, but she was understandably very wary, probably moreso because I was a man. It was obvious that she had been on her own for some time, and had not had the best interactions with humans other than Donita. After a few minutes, though, she let me touch her, and I managed to get a leash on her and loaded both of them into the truck.

Surprisingly, they did not mind Bubba at all, and they settled in very quickly. I decided to head north and drive for as long as I could. We drove several hours, and as the sun began to touch the horizon, I realized I had run out of steam. I took an exit into a town I can't even remember, and stopped at the Super 8 along the interstate. I always used to stay at Super 8's because they allowed dogs when most other hotels didn't.

I checked in, took Bubba in to relax on the bed, and then took crates in and set them up for the girls. Tejas was eager to get out of the truck, and she pottied quickly, so she was in her crate watching TV with Bubba in no time. I knew Lonestar would take longer because of her shyness. I hooked the leash onto her collar and she was more than willing to jump out of the truck. I gave her a pat on the head, and then turned back to do something inconsequential in the front seat of the truck. After a minute or two I commented to

Star that she was being such a good girl for not even pulling on the leash. I turned to give her another petting, and SHE WAS GONE! She had chewed through the nylon leash with ease. The end of the leash looked like it had been sliced by a razor blade.

Star seemed to be very pleased with herself. She stood 30 feet away, 12 inches of leash dangled from her collar, and I swear she was smiling. I panicked! She had been on her own and a stray for so long, would she now just bolt and run in this unknown place? I quickly grabbed the McDonald's bag on the floor by the front seat and calmly said, "Lonestar, want some treats?"

I rattled and crunched the bag, and she took a few steps toward me, and then sat down. I knew right away this would not be easy. There was also the added danger of the motel being located right next to a six lane interstate that was packed with traffic. For the next two hours we danced; Star coming closer, and then almost bolting and running off. I was getting frustrated, so I decided that now that it was dark, I would just sit with my back against a fence in the grass and wait for her to come to me.

She slowly came closer and closer, and then I felt it—a strange burning and unfamiliar feeling in my legs and back. I stayed right where I was, fighting the urge to run around like my hair was on fire. Come on, just a little closer, PLEASE. Finally, she just walked over to me, plopped down, and put her head on my leg. I hooked her to the chain type leash I had so that she could not bite through it again, and then I surveyed the damage. If you're from the south, you know what was happening, but for those of us from the north that don't know, Texas has these sweet little things called FIRE

ANTS, and I had been sitting right on top of their home.

They were all through my clothes and I had bites all over my body. I was starting to not feel so well, so I quickly got Star into the room. I showered and went to bed, but it ended up being a very miserable and restless night for me with all the venom moving through my system. All three dogs, on the other hand, never moved or made a sound. For their first night ever indoors, the girls did great.

After our rough start, the rest of the trip went smoothly. The girls fit right in with the rest of the rescue dogs at my home, and became a part of the family until they could be vetted and adopted into their own forever homes. We figured out that Tejas was about six to eight months old, and her vet visit found her in surprisingly good health. She was cleared for adoption and was adopted just days after being spayed.

Lonestar was a different story. She had some serious internal parasites, and the other scourge of the south, heartworm. She would need to stay with us for an extended time while she received the treatment. At the time, treatment for heartworm was a series of painful injections given in the epaxiel muscles that run along the spine. Many dogs tend to be very sore after the injections, and they also have to be kept absolutely calm for the next eight weeks. They have to stay in their crates—no excitement, running, or playing—with leash walks only as far as the potty, and then back into their crates again.

It was a miserable eight weeks for both Star and us, because we hated confining her so much after all she'd been through, and she didn't understand why she had to stay in there all the time either.

The success rate for this treatment is around 85%, and wouldn't you know it, at the end of her treatment and recheck, Lonestar was part of the 15% that was still heartworm positive. Our poor girl would have to go through the painful treatment all over again after her recovery period from this round.

For the next three months, Star stayed with us as a part of the family and learned to be a proper companion while she recovered. She did well and became incredibly sweet, and—except for the worms—healthy. She was estimated to be between 1-2 years old, so we were hopeful she'd be able to tolerate another round of treatment.

The day came for her retreatment, and she went through it like a champ. It was harder on her the second time, though, and she didn't even want to walk or run with her friends. She slept a lot, and was not our usual happy girl. Six weeks passed slowly for Star, but the good news was that she was finally heartworm free! She was now ready for adoption and another chapter in her exciting life.

For months we screened families and tried to find her the perfect home. We knew she would not be good with cats and small kids, and it seemed like every family that contacted us had either one or both of those deal breakers. We had a few people make the cut to come meet her, but they either did not think she was what they wanted, or she simply didn't like them. At this point, it had been almost a year since bringing her home from Texas.

She really seemed to think she was already home here, and it was during one of our regular morning talks that she made it pretty obvious that she was staying right where she was. Lonestar would sit next to me on the step and I would talk to her and pet her for whatever time I could spare. On this particular morning I asked her if she wanted to stay here and live with us.

She tilted her head as if to say, "What? Are you serious? Is that really a possibility"? I asked her again and it was like a bomb went off inside her. She took off running and butt tucking (it's a lab thing) around the yard, then she came back and started jumping and spinning.

There was no doubt that she understood exactly what I was asking, and she let me know she was staying! Lonestar was finally home, and it was that same morning that she earned her first nickname. After the display she had just given me, she became known as "Circus Dog."

As I write this, it has been eight years since her rescue, and that crazy Circus Dog is still with us. Every day, she runs and jumps and spins in happiness at just being alive. Our best guess is that she is about ten or eleven years old, but she has not slowed down a bit yet. We have gone on to do well over 1000 dog rescues, in every state east of the Rockies. Most were much easier, but a few were even more difficult than the trip to Texas to save two Church Ladies. That's a story for another day.

◌◌

Joe Maringo is the Director of Southwest Pennsylvania Retriever Rescue Org/S.P.A.R.R.O. and Shades of Grey Sanctuary For Senior Dogs in Plum, Pennsylvania. Over the years SPARRO has grown and to date they have rescued over 1,000 dogs, from every single state east of the Rockies and from Canada as well. Donate for their rescue efforts at www.sparro.org.

SPARROW IN THE HOUSE:
Birdie

BY LIZ WOLOSKI

THE TINY BIRD, CUPPED IN MY HAND, whirred its little wings and cheeped with excitement as I propelled a worm-sized bit of hamburger towards the gaping beak. The softness of her feathers and lightness of body was like holding a butterfly. But she wasn't a butterfly, she was a baby house sparrow.

She'd come into my possession when a nearby house was being repaired, and the nest under the eaves was discarded along with two little chicks. I have always been a soft touch when it comes to birds and animals, so the nest and its occupants were presented to me to care for. There was no wildlife rescue or veterinarian to bring them to, so what was I to do? I peered at the two helpless fluff balls with their bright yellow beaks and knew I had to do my best to save them. They were just babies deserving of a chance at life, after all.

I put the nest on a table on our insulated back porch and made a small tent over it with paper towels. They snuggled tightly together and I was confident they were feathered enough to keep warm. I wouldn't give them names because I was not going to get attached. The plan was to feed them until they could fledge and then release them. Simple!

It was obvious from the beginning that one was older and healthier than the other. She was larger, more feathered and much more aggressive, always pushing in front of her nest mate when it was feeding time. And it seemed to always be feeding time. This was a dilemma, as they demanded food every half hour and I had to be at work all day. I also did not know what to feed them, finally deciding raw hamburger would have to suffice for worms.

I awoke an extra hour early for the next few weeks in order to stuff their little bodies before heading to work, worrying all day long about them and hoping they wouldn't die of starvation before I got home. They soon learned the sound of my returning footsteps and would cheep loudly as I climbed the steps to the back door. Then I would spend the rest of the daylight hours feeding them until dusk when they snuggled together contentedly and went to sleep.

The larger chick grew more quickly, despite the fact that I made sure to feed them both equally until they refused anymore food. She was also the tamer of the two. The smaller one gladly devoured the food I sent down his beak but would then retreat to the furthest corner of the nest wanting no further contact with me.

The day came when I arrived home to find them out of the nest—the smaller one perched on a rafter, the larger one flying around the porch and finally landing on my head. My babies were out of the nest! But they were still very dependent on me and the food I provided. I started giving them bread crumbs and offering seed to wean them off the hamburger diet. A few days later I came home to find only the larger of the chicks chirping and flying around my head. I was very sad to discover the sicklier one had died.

My husband and I had begun calling the little sparrow Birdie. Now that she could fly, Birdie took wing from the back porch and into the house. She followed us from room to room chirping loudly, demanding attention, or riding on the back of our dog Skipper, who was a gentle hound and never complained. She flew into the bathroom in the morning as I put on my makeup and groomed my hair. In fact, her favorite pastime was to land on my head and proceed to bathe, crouching low into my hair and whirring her wings like the wild sparrows I've seen taking dust baths in soft dirt. It felt like having a fluffy helicopter on my head.

I also learned she was terrified of the color red. Whenever I wore my red sweater she would fly around terrified and refuse to come near me.

Her beak had grown stronger, the soft yellow showing only in the corners of her mouth. Her feathers were no longer fluff and down but had grown sleek and smooth. As much as I loved her, I knew the time had come for her to fly out into the big wide world and be with her own kind.

One Saturday morning, I walked out the back door with Birdie perched on my shoulder and sat on a lawn chair with my coffee. She was quiet at first, taking in the vista of trees, fences and telephone lines that surrounded our house. I soon became aware of the cacophony of neighborhood sounds, people mowing their lawns, cars driving down the lane, children playing—but most of all I noticed the undercurrent of bird chirps. Birdie heard them too and began to call back to them. Her feathers quivered, she stretched out her neck, and suddenly she flew up into the maple tree.

I called to her and she answered, but she never left her spot on the branch. Suddenly I was terribly afraid. How would she manage all alone in the world? She had no experience of all the hazards that could befall a little bird. I called and called and she peeped back willingly but would not leave her perch. The afternoon passed and friends and neighbors stopped by as I continued to call to the little sparrow.

"How can you tell she's there?" someone asked.

"She's chirping!" I said. "She's calling me."

"There's a lot of birds chirping though."

It was true; there were lots of sparrows in the neighborhood and they had all seemed to gather near our house. But I knew her cheep. I could pick it out of a thousand chirping birds just like a mother knows her child's voice amongst a playground full of children.

We ate supper outside as the sun was setting lower over the horizon. How could I sleep with Birdie all alone on a tree branch outside and afraid to move? A cat or an owl could easily sneak up on her, and I wouldn't be able to save her.

As daylight turned to twilight I called and pleaded to her. She chirped loudly at me and finally, in the last gleam of light, took the brave leap into the air and landed on my head. Then she slid down my hair and nestled safely into the crook of my neck. I felt her scratchy little feet on my skin, her soft feathers against my neck, and stroked her gently, filled with relief and love for the little sparrow.

I was seized with fear. I couldn't let her go out again, it was too dangerous. All the next day she flew around the house and cheeped at the windows. She became excited hearing the wild birds outdoors and kept calling to them. She wanted out but I was too afraid to allow it.

Monday came and I went to work, thinking all day about Birdie. I hurried home and opened the screen door, expecting to hear her chirps and fly to me as she always did—but there was no bird in the porch. Then I heard the sound of her voice, cheeping excitedly, and it was coming from outside!

I stepped out the door and she landed on my head. That's when I noticed a little hole in the screen door that she had somehow managed to squeeze through. "Oh Birdie", I said, and kissed the top of her head.

I brought out some crumbs and sat on the steps watching her eat. She flew up into the tree again but this time when I called her she flew right back to me chattering excitedly, like a child showing off a new skill to her mother. Another sparrow was foraging on the lawn and Birdie flew over to her and began to beg, making herself small by crouching, fluttering her wings, and peeping loudly like she had when she was a little chick. Soon enough she was being fed by the stranger.

When my husband arrived home, he cut away the hole in the screen, enlarging it so she could fly in and out. She happily came in to roost at night, and we'd reached a compromise of sorts. All that summer she had the run of the house and of the neighborhood. Whenever friends visited our yard, Birdie would appear, stealing straws, pecking at jewelry or painted toe nails, and taking her bird baths on visitor's heads.

Getting to work in the morning became a challenge. I'd step out the front door only to have Birdie land on my head. "Shoo!" I'd command. "Go play with your friends."

I'd put my hand under her feet and push her into the air, but she'd refuse to obey and land back on my head, scolding me in return. I began to take her onto the back porch, close the inside door to the house behind me, and run as fast as I could out the front door before she could make her way out the screen and around to the front. If she "won" the race, she'd promptly land on my head again and we'd start the process over. This often went on several times before I could escape.

Sometimes I made it half way down the street before she found me. Once I was at the corner bus stop, about to step on the bus, when she suddenly landed on my head. The bus driver's eyes went wide as I stood there with a sparrow on my head. "Sorry", I sighed, and trudged home with Birdie fluttering above me.

She was always excited to see me at the end of the day when I returned from work. I would take some bread crumbs and toss them around the yard, but she preferred sitting on my hand to eat. Soon her friends began to join in and the fence and lawn would be covered in chirping sparrows. She continued her baby bird begging routine with them and I noticed other sparrows doing the same. It was interesting to witness how the older birds always fed the little beggars no matter that they were all fully grown.

One day I came home and the backyard was literally swarming with sparrows. Our next-door neighbor called to me and joked that we were being invaded. His house was identical to ours, and he opened the door of his back porch as he pointed at his furnace. When he opened the door on the furnace, dozens of sparrows flew out! Fortunately, he was a good man and didn't complain too much.

Many of the birds became quite tame around me, though none so tame as Birdie. When she sat on my hand chattering and eating the crust of bread I held for her, other sparrows would gather close and walk around my feet. The rest of the flock lined the fence or chased the crumbs I tossed to them.

As summer gave way to fall, the leaves on the maple turned yellow, dropping from their branches and blowing across the grass. The flock of sparrows seemed to disburse but Birdie continued to greet me when I returned home from work. As I tossed crumbs into the air, only a few sparrows remained to chase them through the leaves.

Then one day I returned home and she was gone. A few sparrows perched on the fence watching me as I called and called for my little friend. "Where is she?" I asked them, and threw all the crumbs into the air at once in exasperation. I walked around the block calling her. I don't know what people must have thought of the crazy lady wandering around calling to a sparrow, but I didn't care. I just wanted to know she was safe. I walked several blocks in every direction but no little bird landed on my head.

I hardly slept that night. I imagined all kinds of horrors, the worst that she was suffering out there somewhere and I couldn't help her. The second day was a repeat of the first, ending in me wandering the neighborhood calling for Birdie. I left an entire loaf of bread broken into crumbs in case she returned and was hungry.

I was heartbroken, fearing the worse. By the third day I dreaded coming home from work to feel the emptiness of our home without her presence. I walked sullenly into the backyard when suddenly she was on my head, chattering away. "Oh Birdie, where have you been?" I said, sliding my hand under her feet. I was filled with relief and showered her with love and kisses.

She remained with me for a few days, and then she was gone again. I missed her terribly but this time I tried to imagine her off with her friends, enjoying a proper life as the sparrow that she was. Still, I couldn't keep myself from walking the neighborhood and calling to her.

A week later she suddenly appeared again. This time Birdie didn't stay long. I loved her and fussed over her, but knew in my heart it was time for me to finally let her go. She disappeared the next day, and that was the last time I saw her.

I like to think she found her place in a flock, that she mated and raised chicks of her own. Now, many years later, I still think of her with love when I watch the little sparrows at my bird feeder or chasing bread crumbs across the lawn.

I never knew such a little bird could capture such a large chunk of my heart.

ॐॐ

Liz Woloski is an animal lover and lives with her husband and two dogs in a small town in Manitoba. She's written on and off all her life and hopes to devote more time to writing now that she's retired.

Thank you for Joining Us in the Celebration of *Rescue Smiles*. We Hope You Enjoyed the Book!

Could you take a moment to give it a short review on Amazon.com? Your reviews mean the world to our authors, and help them expand their audience and their voice. Thank you so much!

Find links to *Rescue Smiles* and all our great books on Amazon or at www.whochainsyou.com.

Want More? You're in Luck!
More Rescue Smiles
is Now Available!

The heart of the animal rescue world lies in its stories—of freedom, of love, and of sacrifice by those who not only acknowledge but embrace the human-animal bond and its wondrous gifts.

In our second rescue story compilation, Who Chains You Books is pleased to share a glimpse into the emotional lives of animal rescuers and the living beings they hold close. Join us for another helping of heartwarming anecdotes, as Clancy triumphs, Tallulah escapes, Alex survives, and a host of other animals steal our hearts.

Through these stories, you'll get a behind-the-scenes look into the relationships between rescuers and not only dogs and cats, but horses, cows, pigs, birds, and even a ferret, in this delightful second installment of *Rescue Smiles*.

Read more and find links for the book in paperback, kindle, and audiobook at whochainsyou.com.

About the Editor

Tamira Thayne is the author of *The Wrath of Dog, The Curse of Cur, Foster Doggie Insanity,* and *Capitol in Chains,* editor of *More Rescue Smiles,* and the co-editor of *Unchain My Heart* and *Rescue Smiles.* In 2016 she founded Who Chains You, publishing books by and for animal lovers, activists, and rescuers.

In her empathy for the plight of the chained dog, she pioneered the anti-tethering movement in America, forming and leading the nonprofit Dogs Deserve Better for 13 years.

During her time on the front lines of animal activism and rescue she took on plenty of bad guys (often failing miserably); her swan song culminated in the purchase and transformation of Michael Vick's dogfighting compound to a chained-dog rescue and rehabilitation center.

She's spent 878 hours chained to a doghouse on behalf of the voiceless in front of state capitol buildings nationwide, and worked with her daughter to take on a school system's cat dissection program, garnering over 100,000 signatures against the practice.

About the Editor

Heather Leughmyer is the author of *Adopting Adele, The Rat's Guide to Owning a Human, Brave Benny, Courageous Conner, Dandelion's Dream* and *If Your Tears Were Human*, and co-editor of *Rescue Smiles*.

She is also the founder of Happy Endings Rat Rescue, and a graduate of Indiana-Purdue University with a B.A. in Writing and Linguistics.

Writing has been a passion of hers for as long as she has advocated for animals.

She lives in Columbia City, Indiana, with her husband, daughter, and several animal companions.

About Who Chains You Books

WELCOME TO WHO CHAINS YOU: PUBLISHING AND SPIRITUAL MENTORING FOR ANIMAL LOVERS, ACTIVISTS AND ANIMAL RESCUERS.

At Who Chains You Books our mission is a simple one—to amplify the voices of the animals through the empowerment of animal lovers, activists, and rescuers to write and publish books elevating the status of animals in today's society.

We hope you'll visit our website and join us on this adventure we call animal advocacy publishing. We welcome you.

Read more about us at whochainsyou.com.

Also from Who Chains You Books

IT'S ABOUT A
DOG

MAGGIE COUCH

I Once Was Lost
BUT NOW I'M FOUND

DAISY AND THE OLYMPIC
ANIMAL SANCTUARY RESCUE

Laura Koerber

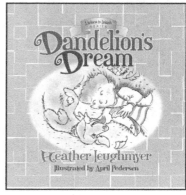

Dandelion's
Dream

Heather Leughmyer
Illustrated by April Pedersen

Tamira Thayne

The
WRATH of DOG

The Chained Gods Series Book 1

And More!
whochainsyou.com

Also from Who Chains You Books

THE DOG THIEF AND OTHER STORIES
BY JILL KEARNEY

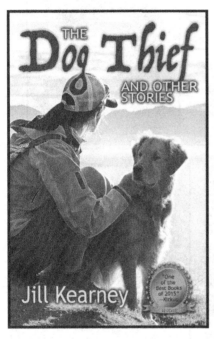

"**D**ecrepit humans rescue desperate canines, cats and the occasional rat in this collection of shaggy but piercing short stories."

Listed by Kirkus Review as one of the best books of 2015, this collection of short stories and a novella explores the complexity of relationships between people and animals in an impoverished rural community where the connections people have with animals are sometimes their only connection to life.

According to Kirkus Review: "Kearney treats her characters, and their relationships with their pets, with a clear-eyed, unsentimental sensitivity and psychological depth. Through their struggles, she shows readers a search for meaning through the humblest acts of caretaking and companionship. A superb collection of stories about the most elemental of bonds."...*Read more and order from whochainsyou.com, Amazon, and other outlets.*

Also from Who Chains You Books

FOSTER DOGGIE INSANITY: TIPS AND TALES
TO KEEP YOUR KOOL AS A DOGGIE FOSTER PARENT
BY TAMIRA CI THAYNE

Have you ever fostered a dog—happy to make a difference—but wondered why you felt frustrated and alone in your experience? Do you want to foster a dog, but don't know where to start, how to prepare, and what to expect? Have you experienced burnout or compassion fatigue in your rescue experience? If so, this is the book for you. Described as "an embrace from a friend who understands what we all go through; it is a beacon of hope to let other rescuers know they are not alone—a must-read for anyone involved in rescue."

This is not a book about dog training, but a book about people training while working with dogs...*Read more and order from whochainsyou.com, Amazon, and other outlets.*

Made in the USA
Monee, IL
19 October 2023

44845339R00095